TEACHING BOWLING

Steps to Success

Robert H. Strickland, MS
Dallas, Texas

Leisure Press
Champaign, Illinois

Library of Congress Cataloging-in-Publication Data

Strickland, Robert.
Teaching bowling—steps to success / Robert H. Strickland.
p. cm.—(Steps to success activity series)
Bibliography: p.
ISBN 0-88011-356-1
1. Bowling—Study and teaching. I. Title. II. Series.
GV903.S773 1989
794.6'07—dc20 89-34382
CIP

ISBN 0-88011-356-1

Developmental Editor: Judy Patterson Wright, PhD
Production Director: Ernie Noa
Copyeditor: Peter Nelson
Assistant Editor: Robert King
Proofreaders: Holly Gilly and Valerie Hall
Typesetter: Yvonne Winsor
Text Design: Keith Blomberg
Text Layout: Kimberlie Henris and Tara Welsch
Cover Design: Jack Davis
Cover Photo: Bill Morrow
Illustrators: Raneé Rogers and Gretchen Walters
Printed By: United Graphics, Inc.

Printed in the United States of America

10 9 8 7 6 5 4 3 2 1

Leisure Press
A Division of Human Kinetics Publishers, Inc.
Box 5076, Champaign, IL 61825-5076
1-800-342-5457
1-800-334-3665 (in Illinois)

Contents

Series Preface

The Steps to Success Activity Series is a breakthrough in skill instruction through the development of complete learning progressions—the *steps to success*. These *steps* help students quickly perform basic skills successfully and prepare them to acquire advanced skills readily. At each step, students are encouraged to learn at their own pace and to integrate their new skills into the total action of the activity, which motivates them to achieve.

The unique features of the Steps to Success Activity Series are the result of comprehensive development—through analyzing existing activity books, incorporating the latest research from the sport sciences, and consulting with students, instructors, teacher educators, and administrators. This groundwork pointed up the need for three different types of books—for participants, instructors, and teacher educators—which we have created and together comprise the Steps to Success Activity Series.

The *participant's book* for each activity is a self-paced, step-by-step guide; learners can use it as a primary resource for a beginning activity class or as a self-instructional guide. The unique features of each *step* in the participant's book include

- sequential illustrations that clearly show proper technique for all basic skills,
- helpful suggestions for detecting and correcting errors,
- excellent drill progressions with accompanying *Success Goals* for measuring performance, and
- a complete checklist for each basic skill for a trained observer to rate the learner's technique.

A comprehensive *instructor's guide* accompanies the participant's book for each activity, emphasizing how to individualize instruction. Each *step* of the instructor's guide promotes successful teaching and learning with

- teaching cues (*Keys to Success*) that emphasize fluidity, rhythm, and wholeness,
- criterion-referenced rating charts for evaluating a participant's initial skill level,
- suggestions for observing and correcting typical errors,
- tips for group management and safety,
- ideas for adapting every drill to increase or decrease the difficulty level,
- quantitative evaluations for all drills (*Success Goals*), and
- a complete test bank of written questions.

The series textbook, *Instructional Design for Teaching Physical Activities*, explains the *steps to success* model, which is the basis for the Steps to Success Activity Series. Teacher educators can use this text in their professional preparation classes to help future teachers and coaches learn how to design effective physical activity programs in school, recreation, or community teaching and coaching settings.

After identifying the need for participant, instructor, and teacher educator texts, we refined the *steps to success* instructional design model and developed prototypes for the participant and the instructor's books. Once these prototypes were fine-tuned, we carefully selected authors for the activities who were not only thoroughly familiar with their sports but had years of experience in teaching them. Each author had to be known as a gifted instructor who understands the teaching of sport so thoroughly that he or she could readily apply the *steps to success* model.

Next, all of the participant's and instructor's manuscripts were carefully developed to meet the guidelines of the *steps to success* model. Then our production team, along with outstanding artists, created a highly visual, user-friendly series of books.

The result: The Steps to Success Activity Series is the premier sports instructional series available today. The participant's books are the best available for helping you to become a master player, the instructor's guides help you to become a master teacher, and the teacher educator's text prepares you to design your own programs.

This series would not have been possible without the contributions of the following:

- Dr. Joan Vickers, instructional design expert,
- Dr. Rainer Martens, Publisher,
- the staff of Human Kinetics Publishers, and
- the *many* students, teachers, coaches, consultants, teacher educators, specialists, and administrators who shared their ideas—and dreams.

Judy Patterson Wright
Series Editor

Preface

Your importance to your students in the *steps to success* approach cannot be overestimated. Effective bowling instructors teach from a systematic, stepwise skill development progression. They understand the mechanics of the delivery and can communicate effectively to students. Good teachers are good observers; they diagnose errors accurately and state corrections clearly to get students back on track quickly. *Teaching Bowling: Steps to Success* will help you develop each of these instructional skills and give you guidelines to individualize your instruction. Drills are designed to enhance student success and to help students troubleshoot errors, set reasonable goals, and practice effectively. Most drills use the buddy system of practice in order to increase time on task and enhance student's observational skills.

The extensive interaction between you and your students provides you an important opportunity to help students learn how to socialize and to enjoy bowling for a lifetime's worth of fun.

This instructor's guide and the participant's book, *Bowling: Steps to Success*, should be in hand for all your instruction, whether you are teaching correct form to beginners or helping skilled bowlers break out of slumps and eliminate bad habits.

It is an honor to have been chosen as an author for the Steps to Success Activity Series. I salute Drs. Rainer Martens, Judy Wright, and Joan Vickers for realizing the need for an effective and systematic method of learning how to bowl and how to teach bowling. I appreciate the extensive attention that Drs. Judy Wright and June Decker gave to revising this instructor's guide. I also give my sincere appreciation to Wilson G. ''Bill'' Taylor for many of the techniques in this book.

Thanks to my wife, Sue, for her loving support, for posing for many of the photographs for the illustrator to work from, and for critically evaluating the manuscript. Thanks to Dr. Will Powers of Ball State University for posing for illustrations, for teaching me his ''Powers Mental Toughness Routine,'' and for allowing me to incorporate portions of the routine into this book. Thanks to Pete Moore, member of the Dallas Bowling Association Hall of Fame, for the loan of special camera equipment, for his always-helpful suggestions, and for proofreading the galleys. Thanks to David Brewster, Myra Lachausse, and Manuel San Miguel for posing for photographs for the illustrator to work from, and for helpful suggestions on how to improve them. Lastly, thanks to Glenn Scrifres for suggesting the term ''low maintenance game.''

Implementing the Steps to Success Staircase

This book is meant to be flexible for not only your students' needs but for your needs as well. It is common to hear that students' perceptions of a task change as the task is learned. However, it is often forgotten that teachers' perceptions and actions also change (Goc-Karp & Zakrajsek, 1987; Housner & Griffey, 1985; Imwold & Hoffman, 1983).

More experienced or master teachers tend to approach the teaching of activities in a similar manner. They are highly organized (e.g., they do not waste time getting groups together or using long explanations); they integrate information (from biomechanics, kinesiology, exercise physiology, motor learning, sport psychology, cognitive psychology, instructional design, etc.); and they relate basic skills into the larger game or performance context, succinctly explaining why the basic skills, concepts, and tactics are important within the game or performance setting. Then, usually within a few minutes, they place their students into realistic practice situations that follow logical manipulations of factors such as

- practicing skills in parts or as a whole,
- adding or removing equipment,
- combining two or more skills,
- bowling for points versus pins,
- using a targeting system, and
- refining timing and coordination.

This book will show you how the basic bowling skills and selected physiological, psychological, and other pertinent knowledge are interrelated (see Appendix A for an overview). You can use this information not only to gain insights into the various interrelationships but also to define the subject matter for bowling. The following questions offer specific suggestions for implementing this knowledge base and help you evaluate and improve your teaching methods, which include class organization, drills, objectives, progressions, and evaluations.

1. Under what conditions do you teach?
   - How much space is available?
   - What type of equipment is available?
   - What is the average class size?
   - How much time is allotted per class session?
   - How many class sessions do you teach?
   - Do you have any teaching assistants?
2. What are your students' initial skill levels?
   - Look for the rating charts located in the beginning of most steps (chapters) to identify the criteria that discriminate between beginning and accomplished skill levels.
3. What is the best order to teach bowling skills?
   - Follow the sequence of steps (chapters) used in this book.
   - See Appendix B.1 for suggestions on when to introduce, review, or continue practicing each step.
   - Based on your answers to the previous questions, use the form in Appendix B.2 to put into order the steps that you will be able to cover in the time available.
4. What objectives do you want your students to accomplish by the end of a lesson, unit, or course?
   - For your technique or qualitative objectives, select from the Student Keys to Success (or see the Keys to Success Checklists in *Bowling: Steps to Success*) that are provided for all basic skills.
   - For your performance or quantitative objectives, select from the Student Success Goals provided for each drill.
   - For written questions on safety, rules, technique, history, and psychological aspects of bowling, select from the Test Bank of written questions.

- See the Sample Individual Program Appendix C.1) for selected technique and performance objectives for a 16-week unit.
- For unit objectives, adjust your total number of selected objectives to fit your unit length (use the form in Appendix C.2).
- For organizing daily objectives, see the Sample Lesson Plan in Appendix D.1, and modify the basic lesson plan form in Appendix D.2 to best fit your needs.

5. How will you evaluate your students?
   - Read the section ''Evaluation Ideas.''
   - Decide on your type of grading system; you could use letter grades, pass-fail, total points, percentages, skill levels (bronze, silver, gold), and so forth.
6. Which activities should be selected to achieve student objectives?
   - Follow the drills for each step because they are specifically designed for large groups of students and are presented in an easy-to-difficult order. Avoid a random approach to selecting drills.
   - Modify drills as necessary to best fit each student's skill level by following the suggestions for decreasing and increasing the difficulty level of each drill.
   - Ask your students to meet the Success Goal listed for each drill.
   - Use the cross-reference to the corresponding step and drill in the participants' book, *Bowling: Steps to Success*, for class assignments or makeups. The bracketed notation [New drill] after a drill title indicates that the drill appears only in this instructor's guide and will be new to your students.
7. What rules and expectations do you have for your class?
   - For general management and safety guidelines, read the section ''Preparing Your Class for Success.''
   - For specific guidelines, read the subhead ''Group Management and Safety Tips'' included with each drill.
   - Let your students know what your rules are during your class orientation or first day of class. Then post the rules and discuss them often.

Teaching is a complex task, requiring you to make many decisions that affect both you and your students (see Figure 1). Use this book to create an effective and successful learning experience for you and everyone you teach. And remember, have fun too!

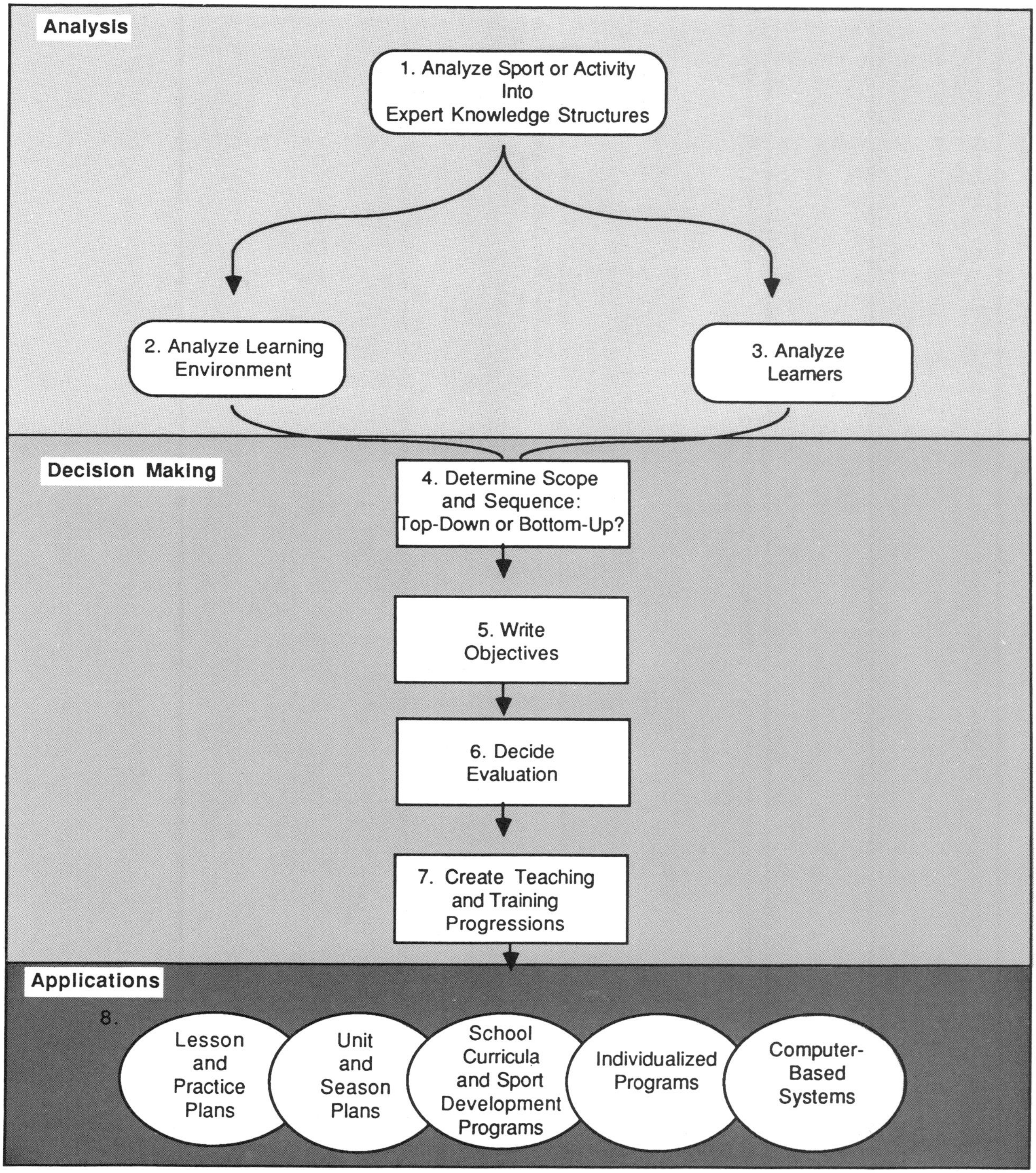

Figure 1 Instructional design model utilizing expert knowledge structures. *Note*. From *Instructional Design for Teaching Physical Activities* by J.N. Vickers, in press, Champaign, IL: Human Kinetics. Copyright by Joan N. Vickers. Reprinted by permission. This instructional design model has appeared in earlier forms in *Badminton: A Structures of Knowledge Approach* (p. 1) by J.N. Vickers and D. Brecht, 1987, Calgary, AB: University Printing Services. Copyright 1987 by Joan N. Vickers; and "The Role of Expert Knowledge Structures in an Instructional Design Model for Physical Education" by J.N. Vickers, 1983, *Journal of Teaching in Physical Education*, **2**(3), p. 20. Copyright 1983 by Joan N. Vickers.

Preparing Your Class for Success

Before you begin teaching your class, you need to make many procedural decisions involving class management, warm-ups and cool-downs, equipment, safety, and liability.

GENERAL CLASS MANAGEMENT

The following items will give you guidance in creating an effective learning environment.

- Review the building's assigned escape route in case of fire or other emergency. You should point out the exits to your class during the safety orientation.
- Check the number of house balls for sufficient variety of weights and house shoes for variety of sizes.
- Check for proper illumination. The lack of proper illumination on the lane targets and approach dots can interfere with learning. Fortunately, this is not a common problem, but it is one about which you should be aware.
- Control the flow of spectators and visitors during class. It may be advantageous to allow students from the next class to quietly observe your class activities, but with the understanding that they will be asked to leave if they disturb anyone.
- Have students keep valuables in lockers or other safe places to avoid potential thefts.
- Keep the pinsetters turned off, if possible, until your students are to begin bowling.
- Begin your presentation after your students have selected balls, changed into bowling shoes, and taken positions in and around the settee area.
- Address the entire class of students from a position at the centermost lane's foul line; attempt eye contact with everyone at one time or another. Use a portable public or house address system if necessary.
- Learn your students' names so you can address them personally. Have them wear name tags for at least the first two or three sessions.
- Assign students often to new working groups to promote socialization and learning.
- If possible, leave the pair of lanes farthest from the exit door open for individual instruction and videotaping.
- Position yourself in the best place to observe the movement. Do not attempt, for example, to evaluate the height of the pushaway from the rear or the lateral alignment of the pushaway from the side. Note that the best observation position is indicated with each error in the "Errors and Corrections" section of each step.
- Check the overhead scores to see if students are keeping score correctly.
- Stress that each student should give the right-of-way to the bowler or bowlers on either side. The objective is to have activity on every other lane at any one time.
- If you are instructing a performer on the approach, signal the other bowlers on the same lane to listen to you as you talk to the performer. This not only helps them learn; it keeps them from occupying themselves unproductively, distracting the performer and possibly disturbing others around them.
- Introduce a maximum of two or three points at a time.
- State only feedback which is closely related to the observed task; as appropriate, use the verbal cues shown in the Student Keys to Success.
- Use objective, positive feedback statements whenever possible. For example, if your student did not keep his or her wrist firm on the previous shot, say "Keep your wrist firmer on your *next* shot!" Avoid saying the negative statement, "You did not keep your wrist firm on your last shot!" A statement like "You never keep your wrist firm" is personally critical, completely unnecessary, and counterproductive.

- Never attempt to give a feedback statement if you did not properly observe the related action. The absence of feedback is better than incorrect feedback; it is always acceptable to say to the performer, "Please repeat the last movement; I did not see it clearly."
- Do not hesitate to stop an entire class and clarify the task objectives if necessary.

CLASS WARM-UPS AND COOL-DOWNS

Following the orientation and lesson presentation for the first two or three classes, and after all questions have been answered, lead the class in the warm-up before beginning the on-lane portion of the lesson. In subsequent class sessions, let the students be responsible for doing the warm-up exercises on their own prior to bowling.

- Demonstrate at the foul line of the centermost lane. Have your students line up on the approach of their lanes, giving themselves plenty of room to bend and stretch. All students should be looking at the instructor. Refer to the participant's book, *Bowling: Steps to Success*, for directions on how to perform the warm-up exercises.
- Caution the class not to mix planes of motion by bending forward or to the side while twisting. Also caution against using deep knee bends.
- Encourage all students to use a cool-down five minutes before leaving the class, especially during cold weather. It is not necessary to lead your class through the cool-down as a group.

EQUIPMENT MANAGEMENT AND SELECTION

Two factors that determine how well a student can bowl are the fit of the grip and the appropriateness of the ball's total weight. If the fit is inappropriate or if the ball is too heavy, all aspects of the delivery, including safety, may be affected.

- Have your students select the proper ball for each class (see the directions for selecting equipment in *Bowling: Steps to Success*). Stress that students should not share a ball.
- Remind your students to return the balls to ball racks where they got them.
- Have your students obtain from the counter supervisor house shoes one-half size smaller than their street shoes. Remind them that comparably numbered sizes differ for men and women.
- Remind the class to return all house shoes to the control counter when finished bowling.
- Encourage your students to choose clothes for bowling that do not interfere with movement during the delivery.
- Remind students that bifocal or trifocal glasses will interfere with the ability to keep their heads up while moving. To avoid making execution and targeting adjustments, these students might try using single vision glasses, if available.
- Remind students to bring their books to each class meeting.

SAFETY PRECAUTIONS

Read the following safety precautions aloud to your class on the first day and post a copy in a conspicuous place.

- Be aware of where you are and how much room you have to make any movements.
- Take a warm-up to avoid injury.
- Take practice swings or slides only on the approach and in the direction of the pins. (This may not be practical when you are selecting a ball for use.)
- Look in the direction where you are walking.
- Carry your ball in front of you—never dangling at your side—while walking.
- Check your bowling shoes and the approach for potentially dangerous objects or substances before bowling.
- Pick up your ball from the ball return only after it has come to a stop on the ball return and with your hands on both sides to avoid overtiring your bowling hand and arm, and to avoid smashed toes and fingers.

- Look down at the ball while you are picking it up!
- Take a *test slide* to the foul line before actually delivering a ball. The test slide is simply an approach taken slowly, without a ball, and ending with a slide at the foul line. Anyone taking a test slide should anticipate the sliding foot sticking so he or she will not fall if this occurs.
- Check your shoes after you have walked outside of the settee area.
- Never take food or drinks into the settee area.
- Never bowl in street shoes.
- Don't apply powder or ashes to the approach to facilitate sliding. Inform the control counter person that the approach needs to be conditioned.
- Don't step beyond the foul line; this can result in lane dressing being tracked back onto the approach.
- Never trigger a pinsetting machine to operate if someone is working on it.
- Never roll a ball toward the pins if someone is working on the pinsetter or if the pins are not fully exposed and ready for the ball to be rolled.

PRECLASS CHECKLIST

The following is a list of activities that need your attention prior to a class.

- Prepare handouts, visual materials, and so forth.
- Decide the least time-consuming method you can use for taking roll. For example, you may check roll as you move from lane to lane during class or you may have students report directly to you after they have their equipment and are ready to bowl.
- Make sure you have adequate scoresheets and pencils.
- Each day decide whether you will be shadow bowling or using pins.
- Determine how many students will be assigned to each lane, and decide how they will be assigned.
- Check the approaches for moisture or excessive slippage. Have any problems corrected or flagged before the class begins.

POSTCLASS CHECKLIST

The following is a list of activities that need your attention after a class.

- Check after each class period to make sure that students have returned all equipment to the proper places.
- Pick up pencils and scoresheets after each class.

LIABILITY CHECKLIST

There are eight legal duties owed by a bowling instructor to the students of a course to fulfill the obligations of liability.

1. Adequate Supervision

As an instructor, you must provide adequate supervision to protect students from inherent or extraneous hazards of the situation. Keep your eyes and ears open at all times for reckless student activity. Some persons feel the necessity to show off, making comic deliveries of the ball, walking across several approaches, and so forth. Do not allow such activity to continue.

2. Sound Planning

You must also provide sound planning for the activities being conducted. Plan for a smooth, uncongested flow of human traffic during class; avoid creating situations in which too many persons are on one lane or in which many persons are carrying balls around at the same time.

3. Inherent Risks

The inherent risks of bowling are discussed in ''Safety Precautions'' in an earlier section. You have a duty to your students to warn them adequately of risks and to be sure that they understand those risks.

4. Safe Environment

A safe environment also includes the area surrounding the lanes. Inspect the ball returns, scorekeeping units, settee seats, and spectator seats for loose bolts, sharp protrusions, or cracks. Check the floor for spills, loose tiles, holes, and hazardous protrusions.

5. Evaluating Students' Fitness for the Activity

This aspect is not as critical to bowling as it is for other, more vigorous activities. However, you should make each student's existing physical condition part of your records, noting any condition which may cause pain, injury, or inability to perform certain movements in class so you may compensate for the individual's problems.

6. Emergency First Aid Procedures

In the event of an accident, you must be prepared to provide adequate medical assistance. It is your duty to your students to have planned, posted medical procedures that can be put immediately into action. In addition, you must know how to immediately summon the aid of an available doctor, nurse, or paramedic; have their phone numbers with you at all times. Failure to provide this protection can result in a court finding of negligence.

7. Other Legal Concerns

You cannot restrict your classes or your students in a way that violates their civil rights. Your legal duty is to provide for the legal rights and concerns of your students, staff, and any spectators allowed into the class.

8. General Legal Concerns

In today's lawsuit-happy environment, you must be aware of all the possibilities for liability and must take adequate measures to protect yourself. Always keep accurate records of your activities, especially in the event of an accident involving an injury. Keep such records for a minimum of 5 years. It is a wise practice for all instructors to carry adequate personal liability insurance. Rates for insurance have risen dramatically in recent years, but you should consider very seriously the consequences of being uninsured.

Step 1 Setup

A student must master the *setup*, often referred to as the *stance* or the *address*, to achieve good balance and superior control of the body's center of gravity during movement, resulting in greater bowling accuracy.

Even though the setup is the easiest bowling element to master, your students will show some variety of skill levels, even within the same class. You should immediately develop a critical eye for observing differences in their setup positions. Use the following setup criteria as observation and evaluation tools, or select any descriptors in the ''Setup Keys to Success Checklist'' (see *Bowling: Steps to Success*, the participant's book), which describes proper technique. Generally, you will find two skill levels—beginning and accomplished.

STUDENT KEYS TO SUCCESS

- Alert, standing tall
- Squared feet, hips, and shoulders
- Back upright, head high
- Ball in line with bowling arm

Setup Rating

CRITERION	BEGINNING LEVEL	ACCOMPLISHED LEVEL
Preparation	• Picks up ball in any manner • Does not check for clearance	• Picks up ball correctly • Always checks for clearance
Execution	• Stands anywhere on approach • Appears loose, sloppy • Not squared up	• Always takes correct setup location on approach • Creates impression of concentrating on a target • Very square and still

Error Detection and Correction for the Setup

A well-constructed setup—essential for an effective pushaway and a well-balanced delivery—should give the impression of squareness, stability, and stillness.

As you observe your students, you will find that the most typical setup errors are the lack of the ball's alignment with the bowling arm, not holding the back upright, not keeping the feet apart and even with each other, allowing the bowling shoulder to drop, and allowing the knees to bend. These factors interfere with squareness and stability both prior to movement and during the delivery, giving the bowler an overall loose appearance.

All these errors are equally important. Furthermore, most of the errors are not readily recognized by the bowler. If you find one of these errors, refer to the right-hand side of the page to find out how to correct it. If you find more than one error, correct one at a time, starting with the feet and working upward. To quicken your pace, use the following error observation sequence.

ERROR | **CORRECTION**

Take a position behind the student to check for Errors 1 through 4.

1. The heel of the sliding foot is not at the proper setup location.
   - **Correction:** 1. Have student place the inner edge of the sliding foot on the first dot to the outside of the large center dot.
2. The swingside foot is behind the sliding foot.
   - **Correction:** 2. Make sure that the student's toes and heels form a square.

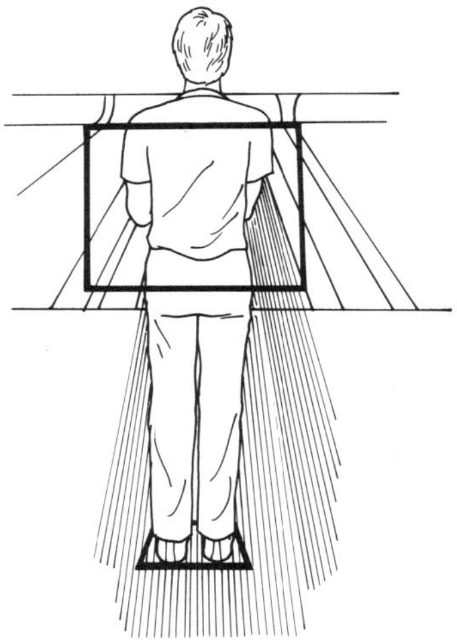

ERROR	CORRECTION
3. The bowling shoulder appears lower than the other shoulder.	3. Have student keep both shoulders level, parallel with the floor.
4. The performer is shaking or fidgeting during the final portion of the setup.	4. Ask student to remain very still, take a deep breath, and let it out slowly.
Move to the student's swingside to check for Errors 5 through 7.	
5. One or both knees are bent.	5. Have student straighten the knees just short of the locked position.
6. The body appears to be twisted, the bowling shoulder farther back than the other.	6. Have student square the shoulders to the hips and hold the bowling elbow even with the ribcage (see Correction 2).
7. The body leans more than 20 degrees forward, or the head or shoulders are too far forward.	7. Ask student to visualize him- or herself standing tall in a vertical plane. Suggest word cues like ''be snooty,'' explaining that it means to look out of the bottoms of the eyes.
Move to a position directly in front of the student to check for Errors 8 and 9.	
8. The ball is held either too low and too close to the center of the body, or too far away from the body.	8. Recommend the Alignment Awareness Drill (Drill 3), which exphasizes holding the ball in line with the shoulder and the target, the wrist higher than the elbow.
9. Too much of the ball's weight is in the bowling arm.	9. Have student place the balance hand under the bowling hand and lift very slightly with the balance hand. Then practice the Bowling Arm Tension Awareness Drill (Drill 4).

Setup Drills

1. *Check Sequence Run-Through*

[Corresponds to *Bowling*, Step 1, Drill 1]

Group Management and Safety Tips

- A ratio of one observing student to one performer is preferred. The drill should be performed on the approach. Ideally, two students stand on each lane, the observer in front or to the side of the performer.
- This is a good opportunity to stress the necessity of the performer being aware of those on nearby lanes and exercising proper courtesy.
- As you move through the class checking for quality of the setup position, note the distance between a student's feet. If the feet are too close together, use the "trick" detailed in the Off-Balance Push Drill, (Drill 5), to dramatize the lack of stability.

Instructions to Class

- "Using a sequence of checks will help you accurately and quickly execute the setup."
- "Study the Setup Keys to Success in Figure 1.1 in your book thoroughly. Using your ball, act out each key as you recite your intentions to your partner, who will check you and compute your score."
- "To begin, carefully take your ball from the ball return and place it in your nonbowling, or balance, hand to avoid unnecessary tension in your bowling arm."
- "Stand approximately 2 feet from the end of the approach and look at the set of dots closest to you. From this *next-up position*, check for clearance of bowlers to either side and step up onto the approach to begin your setup ritual."
- "Place the inner edge of the sole of your sliding foot on the dot 5 boards to the *outside* (to your *swingside*—the side of the lane on your bowling-arm side) of the large center dot of either set of approach dots."
- "Next check to make sure that your toes and heels form a square, and that your toes are pointed straight ahead toward your target—the second arrow from the swingside channel. Ensure that your knees are straight, your hips and shoulders parallel with each other and perpendicular to the feet, and your back upright with your head high—*be snooty*!"
- "Here is a mental picture: Pretend the bottoms of your eyes are emitting laser beams that are burning a hole in the second arrow."
- "Finally, put your fingers in the gripping holes and transfer your ball to a position in line with your bowling arm and the second arrow. Keep your forearm slightly up and hold most of the ball's weight in your balance arm, not your bowling arm. Focus more strongly on the second arrow, take a deep breath, exhale, and hold your stomach in."
- "Remain steady, with your mind relatively quiet, and concentrate. Do not fidget or waggle the ball."

Student Options

- "With a partner, decide whether you want to alternate or complete all trials consecutively."

- ''After practicing, ask your partner to observe and analyze your setup according to the Setup Keys to Success checklist in your book.''

Student Success Goal

- Recite and perform all Setup Keys to Success (a perfect score) in 5 or fewer attempts

To Decrease Difficulty

- Let student recite the Setup Keys to Success for only one phase at a time.
- Allow liberal partner prompting.
- Allow use of a lighter ball.

To Increase Difficulty

- Prohibit partner prompting.

2. *Balance Awareness*

[Corresponds to *Bowling*, Step 1, Drill 2]

Group Management and Safety Tip

- A ratio of one student observer to one performer is preferred. This drill should be performed on the approach. The observer can stand in front or to the side of the performer, depending on the direction of the performer's lean.

Instructions to Class

- ''Focus your attention on the quality of your body balance by comparing off-balance body positions (either too far forward or sideward) to the vertical.''
- ''First, from the completed setup position, lean forward slowly, shifting your weight to the balls of your feet. Lean forward just enough to feel that you are about to lose your balance. Return to the initial upright position.''
- ''Next lean to the swingside, paying attention to the weight distribution on your feet. Lean swingside just enough to feel your sliding (balance-side) foot lift off the approach. Return to the upright position.''
- ''Repeat both types of leans, alternating off-balance, then in-balance, with your eyes open and closed. Concentrate on finding the feeling of balance—neither too far forward nor backward, and neither too far to the swingside nor to the nonswingside.''

Student Options

- ''With a partner, decide whether you want to alternate or complete all trials consecutively.''
- ''After practicing, ask your partner to observe and analyze your setup according to the Setup Keys to Success Checklist in your book.''

Student Success Goal

- 20 total lean comparisons
  a. With eyes open
     5 comparisons of forward leans, balance
     5 comparisons of swingside leans, balance
  b. With eyes closed
     5 comparisons of forward leans, balance
     5 comparisons of swingside leans, balance

To Decrease Difficulty

- Allow use of a lighter ball.

To Increase Difficulty

- Do more sequences with eyes closed.

3. *Alignment Awareness*

[Corresponds to *Bowling*, Step 1, Drill 3]

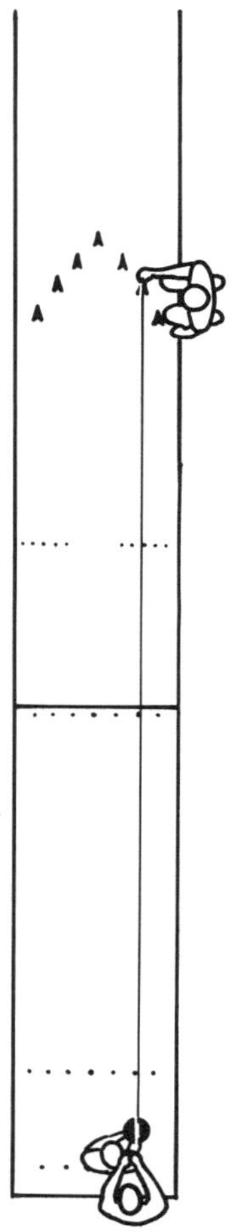

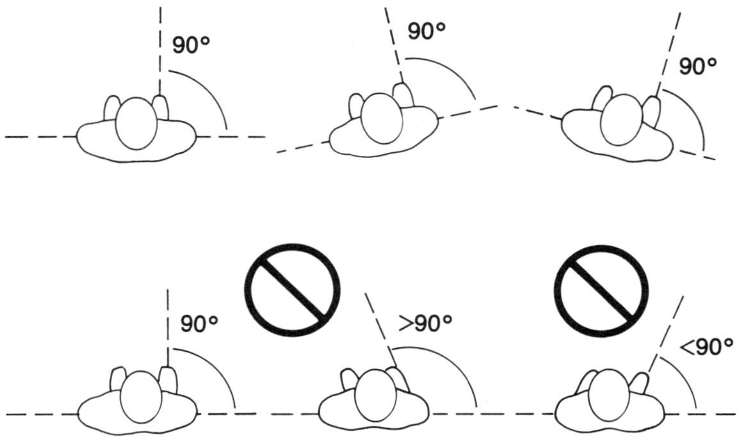

Group Management and Safety Tips

- Run a string from the center of the student's shoulder joint, over the center of the bowling ball, and to the second arrow to illustrate the relationship of the three points and the perpendicular angle of this line to the shoulders.
- Stress that "pointing the feet" means turning the center of the entire body in the direction the feet are pointed. Don't let students twist only at the waist or move only their feet to accomplish this—they must reposition their entire body.

Equipment

- String, 30 foot lengths per lane
- Yardsticks, 1 or 2 optional

Instructions to Class

- "This drill focuses your attention on how well you and your ball are aligned with the second arrow."
- "In your completed setup position, look at your swingside shoulder, then at the ball, and finally at the second arrow. Move your ball so that the three—shoulder, ball, arrow—lie along an imaginary straight line perfectly perpendicular to your shoulders."
- "Next, without moving your heels, point your toes 3 inches to the outside and check the alignment of your shoulder, your ball, and the second arrow. Then return to your correctly aligned position."
- "Next, point your toes 3 inches to the inside and repeat the same checks, again noting the loss of alignment and returning to the correctly aligned position."

Student Option

- "Ask a partner to place a yardstick horizontally so it is supported by the center of your shoulder joint and the top center of the ball. Have the partner look down the yardstick from behind, as if aiming a gun. Your partner can tell you if your shoulder and the ball are in line with the target."

Student Success Goal

- 10 total comparisons of misalignment with correct alignment

  5 outside misalignments with correct alignments

  5 inside misalignments with correct alignments

To Decrease Difficulty

- Not applicable.

To Increase Difficulty

- Not applicable.

4. *Bowling Arm Tension Awareness*

[Corresponds to *Bowling*, Step 1, Drill 4]

Group Management and Safety Tip

- Inform your students to rest during this drill if their bowling arms become fatigued.

Instructions to Class

- "A final setup check is to focus your attention on the amount of tension in your bowling arm. This extremely important concept will have a great influence on your ability to generate a free-pendulum swing."
- "While in your setup position, tense your bowling hand and arm, squeezing your grip on the ball, and carrying the majority of the ball's weight in your bowling arm. Alternate this action with a conscious reduction of tension in your bowling hand and arm."
- "Here is a mental picture: Visualize your forearm and upper arm becoming less tense as you eliminate the grip's excess squeezing yet keep your wrist firm."
- "Next transfer all of the weight of the ball into your balance hand and arm. Simply hold your ball in the grip; do not squeeze it. Note the contrast between sensations as you alternately tense and relax your bowling arm, and how each action affects the tension in your back and shoulders."
- "Repeat this until you feel all of the weight of the ball being carried by your balance hand and arm, and your bowling hand holding, not squeezing, the ball."

Student Option

- "You may allow a partner to feel your forearm and biceps to give you verbal feedback to go with the feel."

Student Success Goal

- 20 total actions, 10 tense biceps alternating with 10 relaxed biceps

To Decrease Difficulty

- Without a ball, have student tense the hand and arm by squeezing very tightly first, then releasing.
- Allow use of a lighter ball.

To Increase Difficulty

- Have student hold the tension 5 to 10 seconds before relaxing.

5. *Off-Balance Push Drill*

[New Drill]

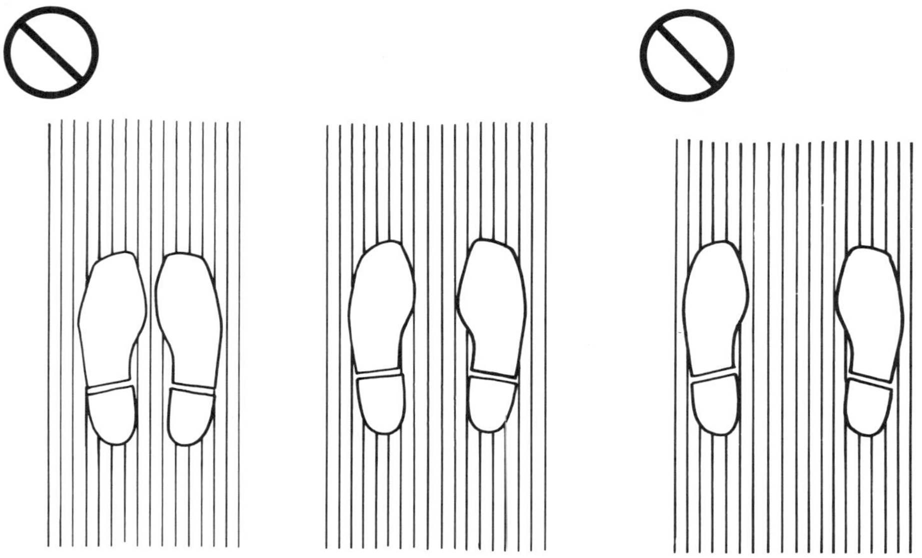

Group Management and Safety Tips

- This is an optional drill that pointedly demonstrates the need for sufficiently wide placement of the feet in the setup to ensure a stable base of support. It is appropriate for students who need additional instruction or for advanced students who desire more information.
- You have an active role in this drill. Stand facing your student, who is set up on the approach. Gently try to push him or her off balance to either side by pushing laterally with your fingers on one shoulder. Notice your student's astonishment to be pushed off balance so easily.
- Then, instruct the student to space the feet 3 or more inches apart in the setup, while you again attempt the off-balance push. You both will see that it is more difficult, if not impossible, to push the student off balance with the broader base of support resulting from the wider stance.

Instructions to Individual

- "Assume your setup with your feet close together. Concentrate on your target and pretend that you are almost ready to begin movement."
- "Watch what happens to your balance when I gently push on your shoulder."
- "Now assume a stance with your feet 3 or 4 inches apart. As before, concentrate on your target and pretend that your movement is almost ready to begin."
- "Again, notice what happens to your balance. Which position is most stable?"

Student Option

- "Once you understand how, work with a partner, taking turns checking each other's balance."

Student Success Goal

- Demonstrate a well-balanced setup

To Decrease Difficulty

- Not applicable.

To Increase Difficulty

- Not applicable.

Step 2 Pendulum Swing

The pendulum swing is the most important aspect of bowling because it affords the best opportunity to maintain a consistent rhythm around which the entire approach and delivery is built. The arm's free-pendulum swing acts like a timing governor on a machine, like the pendulum on a grandfather's clock, which ensures that seconds, minutes, and hours are consistent intervals.

Muscular force is not desirable, because it will speed up or slow down the swing, making the timing to which the footwork must be matched inconsistent. The ball should simply fall into the downswing from the extended pushaway position and into the forward swing from the top of the backswing, in both cases drawn only by the force of gravity—''gravity down, gravity up!''

Although not difficult to learn, the pendulum swing is affected by stress in the bowler; hence, it is more difficult to master and monitor than the setup. Therefore, your students will probably display a wide variety of skill levels. Because differences in muscle tension in the swing are difficult to detect, you must work hard to develop a quick, critical eye for observing variations among the ways in which your students attempt their pendulum swings.

STUDENT KEYS TO SUCCESS

- Body squared and stable
- Ball falls into swing
- Body stable as ball swings
- Body stable as ball stops

Pendulum Swing Rating

CRITERION	BEGINNING LEVEL	ACCOMPLISHED LEVEL
Preparation	• Elbow bent • Shoulders not square to partner	• Elbow straight • Shoulders square to partner
Execution	• Keeps ball from falling into arc • Upper body pulled forward and down by weight of ball • Moves upper body to move ball on down-back-up cycle	• Allows ball to fall into arc • Shoulders stable • Lets ball swing up freely on return to partner
Recovery	• Upper body leans over • Shoulders not square • Elbow bent	• Upper body erect • Shoulders square to partner • Elbow still straight

Error Detection and Correction for the Pendulum Swing

A properly directed free-pendulum swing appears to be relatively effortless. However, to the untrained eye, even a retarded, hurried, or misaligned swing may appear to be correct. Look for the following errors in particular.

ERROR	CORRECTION
Take a position behind the student; direct your attention over the bowling shoulder, in line with the ball; and check for Error 1.	
1. The swing arm is not perpendicular to the shoulders.	1. Have student square the arm to the shoulders.

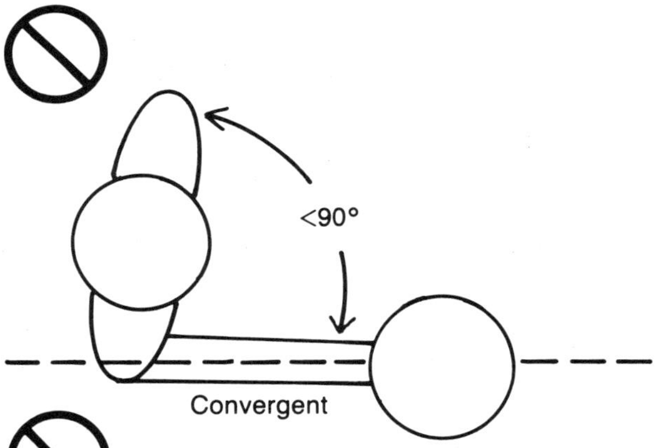

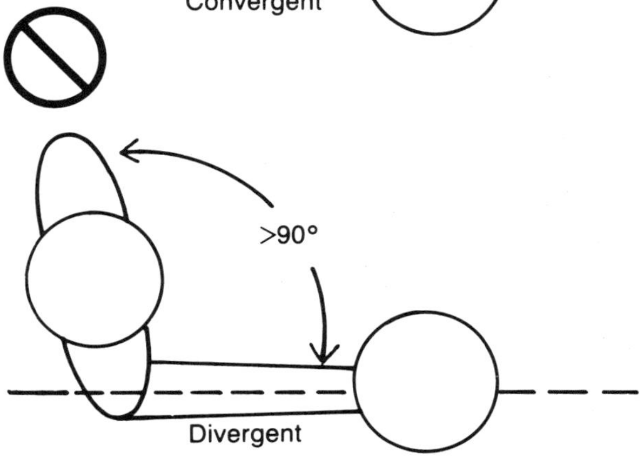

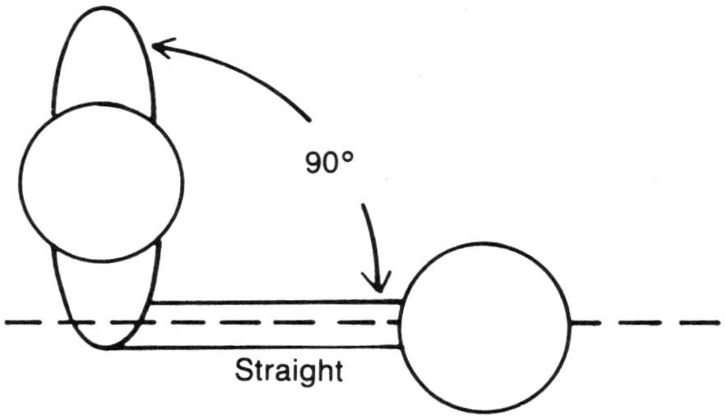

ERROR ⃠ **CORRECTION**

Move to the student's swingside to check for Errors 2 through 5.

2. The bowling elbow is bent.
3. The wrist appears too loose.
4. The ball appears to be swinging slower or faster than a free pendulum.
5. Grip loosens as ball starts into the downswing.

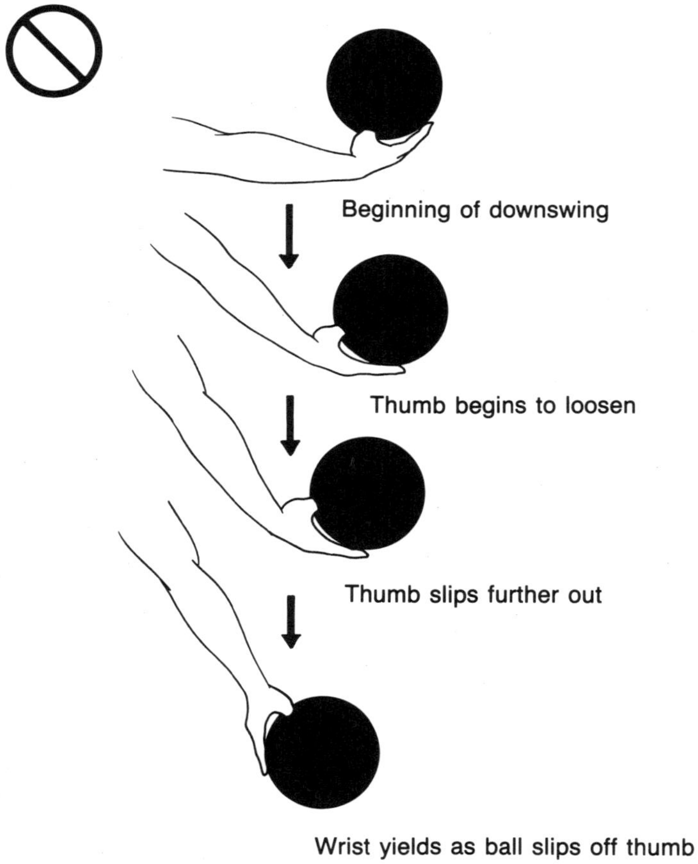

2. Ask student to extend the elbow and try to feel the gravitational pull on the ball.
3. Have student firm, or straighten, the wrist.
4. Use the cue words ''let the ball fall'' into the swing. Recommend the Muscling Awareness Drill (Drill 2).
5. Check the ball's fit and weight, and replace it with a fit and weight more appropriate for the student.

Pendulum Swing Drills

1. *Free Swing Cadence*

[Corresponds to *Bowling*, Step 2, Drill 1]

Group Management and Safety Tips

- This and the following drills are performed with student pairs face-to-face, one partner starting and stopping the other's swing. Before each drill, remind your students to swing only in line with the approach, never at an angle to it. They should always check behind them before swinging balls. Remind them to warn their partners to keep their faces and hands clear of the swings, and to stop the swings only with their hands on the sides of the balls.
- The objectives of this drill are to develop a feel for proper swing alignment and to determine the cadence that sets delivery timing.
- This is a good time to check each student's ball fit. The student may find it impossible to swing the ball freely due to lack of grip security, tending to lose the grip as the ball starts into the downswing. The ball may be improperly fit, too heavy, or both (see Error 5). Replace the ball with one better suited to the student.

Instructions to Class

- ''Take a normal setup position with your partner on the approach facing you and about 3 feet away.''
- ''Push your ball straight out in front of your shoulder and into your partner's hands.''
- ''Drop your balance arm to your side, giving the ball's weight to your partner. You are now in the extension setup position.''
- ''When you're ready, close your eyes and say 'one'.''
- ''Partners, let the ball drop into its swing when you hear 'one'.''
- ''Do not slow down or speed up the ball. Let gravity do the work.''
- ''Partners, say 'two' when the ball passes the bowler's swingside leg.''
- ''Say 'three' when the ball is at the top of the backswing.''
- ''Say 'four' when the ball passes the swingside leg again.''

Student Option

- ''Try opening your eyes to check that you can still sense the ball's position and timing during the count.''

Student Success Goal

- 10 consecutive free-pendulum swings

To Decrease Difficulty

- Have student do more free swings with eyes closed.
- Allow use of a lighter ball.

To Increase Difficulty

- Let student alternately close, then open eyes.

2. *Muscling Awareness*

[Corresponds to *Bowling*, Step 2, Drill 2]

Group Management and Safety Tips

- This drill is best accomplished with students working one on one.
- Repeat the safety precautions regarding the swing (see Drill 1).

Instructions to Class

- ''Now you are ready to learn how to troubleshoot your swing. The purpose of this drill is to intentionally modify your swing speed by muscular force so that you can understand how it feels to muscle the ball two ways, slowing down and speeding up.''
- ''Assume the extension setup, with your partner assisting you as in the previous drill. To feel a retarded swing, let your partner know what you are doing, then deliberately tense your arm by slightly lifting up a little of the weight of the ball while it is still in your partner's hands. Close your eyes and say 'one,' to signal your partner to release the ball. Keep your arm in this slightly tense state during the entire swing. Focus your attention on the tension in your arm.''
- ''Note the speed of the ball while your partner continues to count the cadence. Repeat this part of the drill 9 times, lifting more of the ball's weight out of your partner's hands each time, until you have lifted the ball completely off your partner's hands before you start your swing. Score the relative differences in swing speed you feel.''
- ''To feel an accelerated swing, let your partner know what you are doing, then deliberately pull the ball down slightly while it is still in your partner's hands. Close your eyes and say 'one.' Keep your arm in this tense state throughout the swing.''
- ''Note the speed of the swing while your partner continues to count the cadence. Repeat this part of the drill 9 times, pulling down more each time, adding slightly to the ball's weight in your partner's hands before you start your swing. Score the relative differences in swing speed you feel.''

Student Options

- ''You and your partner can agree to mix the three varieties of swing tensions—retarded, forced, and correct.''
- ''You can decide the order to use in a given trial but not tell your partner. Then, ask your partner to identify which swing tension was used.''

Student Success Goal

- 18 total swings from an extended setup position

  9 retarded swings

  9 accelerated swings

To Decrease Difficulty

- Allow use of a lighter ball.

To Increase Difficulty

- Have student alternately contrast the tension necessary for an incorrect (retarded or forced) with the correct swing tension.

3. *Hoist and Clip Awareness*

[Corresponds to *Bowling*, Step 2, Drill 3]

Group Management and Safety Tips

- This drill is best accomplished with students working one on one.
- Repeat the safety precautions regarding the swing (see Drill 1).

Instructions to Class

- "The goals of this drill are to practice two errors, a hoist and a clip, so that you can ultimately recognize any tendencies to make these errors, and correct them. Neither error is as distinct in this drill as when a full approach is taken."
- "A *hoist* is the act of pulling the ball up into the backswing with the muscles of the back of the arm, the shoulder, and the back; it is not a free swing. A hoist is usually caused by a low, late pushaway and a retarded swing—the most common causes of late ball timing."
- "In an extended setup position, have your partner hold your ball 2 feet lower than usual. This should place the ball at a level between your waist and knees. Do not lean over; remain erect. When you signal to begin the swing by saying 'one,' let the ball swing freely. Focus on the tendency to hoist, or lift up, the ball behind you, while your partner completes the cadence. Alternate 3 hoists with 3 free-pendulum swings for comparison."
- "A *clip* is the act of stopping the backswing short with the muscles of the shoulder and upper arm before it reaches the top of the backswing. A clip may be caused by a high or early pushaway, or limited flexibility of the shoulder."
- "Repeat the drill with your partner holding your ball 1 foot higher than usual, putting the ball above the level of your shoulders. Remain erect. When you signal to begin the swing by saying 'one,' let the ball swing freely. Focus on the tendency to stop the ball short in your backswing, while your partner completes the cadence. Alternate 3 clips with 3 free-pendulum swings for comparison."

Student Options

- "Periodically, close your eyes to better sense the ball's position during the count."
- "You and your partner can agree to mix the three swing heights—hoisted, clipped, and normal."
- "In pairs, the performer determines which height to use in a given trial but does not inform the assisting partner, who then identifies which height is used."

Student Success Goals

- 3 hoist and free-pendulum swing comparisons
- 3 clip and free-pendulum swing comparisons

To Decrease Difficulty

- Allow use of a lighter ball.
- Have student close eyes to focus on feel of errors as compared to the feel of the correct pendulum swing.

To Increase Difficulty

- Have student alternately close, then open eyes.

4. *Swing Alignment Awareness*

[Corresponds to *Bowling*, Step 2, Drill 4]

Group Management and Safety Tips

- This drill is best done by pairs of students working one on one.
- Repeat the safety precautions regarding the swing (see Drill 1).

Instructions to Class

- ''Repeat the previous drill, only focus on two errors in swing plane alignment that may affect your body's stability.''
- ''To feel the bumpout (convergent) swing, have your partner hold your ball 6 to 8 inches farther to the inside than in the ideal extension setup position, placing the ball directly in front of the midline of your body. Remain squared otherwise; do not turn your bowling shoulder inward.''
- ''When you signal to begin the swing by saying 'one,' let the ball swing freely. Focus on the ball pulling you off balance to the back and toward your swingside. This pulling is even more distinct now than when a full approach is taken, because then one or more steps would be taken in the opposite direction to regain control of your body's center of gravity. Later, you will find that the bumpout swing can cause you to miss your target to the inside. Alternate 3 bumpout swings with 3 properly directed swings for comparison.''
- ''To feel a wraparound (divergent) swing, have your partner hold your ball 6 to 8 inches farther to the outside than the ideal extension setup position. Again, remain squared otherwise; do not turn your bowling shoulder outward.''
- ''When you signal to begin the swing by saying 'one,' let the ball swing freely. Focus on the tendency of the ball to pull you off balance to the front and to the outside of your swing. This error is also more distinct now than when a full approach is taken. Later, you will find that the wraparound swing can cause you to miss your target to the outside. Alternate 3 wraparound swings with 3 properly directed swings for comparison.''

Student Options

- ''Close your eyes to better sense the ball's position during the count.''
- ''You and your partner can agree to mix the three swings—bumpout, wraparound, and normal.''
- ''In pairs, the performing partner determines which deviation to use in a given trial but does not inform the assisting partner, who then identifies which swing is used.''

Student Success Goals

- 3 bumpout and free-pendulum swing comparisons
- 3 wraparound and free-pendulum swing comparisons

To Decrease Difficulty

- Allow use of a lighter ball.
- Let student close eyes to feel comparisons.

To Increase Difficulty

- Let students lean forward during the various swings to see the effect on swing alignment. A 45 to 60 degree bend will make the bumpout error occur more easily. Postural errors may occur in isolation or in combination with swing misalignments. Student awareness of these errors facilitates self-correction now and later, when footwork is added.

Step 3 Footwork

Emphasize that the student must fit the footwork to the swing—not the other way around!

Proper footwork uses heel-toe steps, generally the same as a person's normal walking gait. Shuffling steps are not desirable because they are more difficult to keep in time, and they promote bending the legs before the last step and slide, resulting in a squatting, ''duck-walk'' walking pattern. Stress also that all the steps should be taken at the same speed; the student should not speed up when nearing the foul line.

Footwork is easy to master when the element of the swinging ball is removed as it is throughout Step 3. Your students will typically display a narrower variety of skill levels with footwork than with other skills, but you should still sharpen your ability to observe differences.

STUDENT KEYS TO SUCCESS

- Upright and squared before movement
- Ball at midline
- Heel-toe steps in cadence
- Slide to sitting-tall finish

Footwork Rating

CRITERION	BEGINNING LEVEL	ACCOMPLISHED LEVEL
Preparation	• Shoulders not square • Ball not held in midline position • Knees bent or elbows flared out	• Shoulders square • Ball at midline • Elbows held in, back and knees straight
Execution	• Steps forward on toe • Leans upper body forward • Bends knees before third step	• Steps out on heel • Back and knees straight, ball held at midline • Knee bend begins after third step
Recovery	• Leans forward, off balance or shaky • Knees not sufficiently bent	• Back straight • Knees bent deeply, obvious sitting posture • Ball at midline

Error Detection and Correction for Footwork

Footwork errors during an actual delivery usually result from an error in timing (in rhythm) between the ball and the footwork through an improperly directed pushaway, which will be covered in Step 10. At this point, the most common errors are an unstable gait and a condition called fast feet, because the footwork outruns the swing. Your students will typically err in the way they take their steps to the foul line. Look for the following errors in particular.

ERROR	CORRECTION
Take a position either behind or to the swing-side of the student to check for Errors 1 through 5.	
1. Steps are taken too fast.	1. Tell your student to start counting the swing cadence prior to fitting the steps to the cadence (see Drill 2).
2. Either the first step or the entire approach is taken on the toes or with a shuffle.	2. Use cue words ''heel, toe, walk tall.'' Recommend the Full Footwork and Cadence Drill (Drill 2).
3. The heels are touching down too abruptly, with the soles of the shoes slapping.	3. Ask student to check that the knees do not lock when walking normally to the line.

ERROR

4. The head "bobbles" during the first three steps because the knees bend too much on count "two."

CORRECTION

4. Have student do heel-toe steps in cadence, and concentrate on staying level until after count "three."

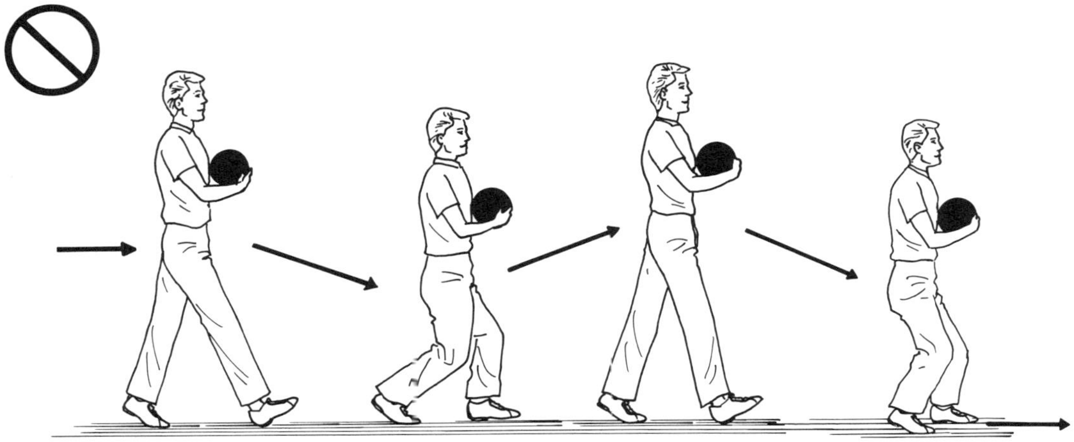

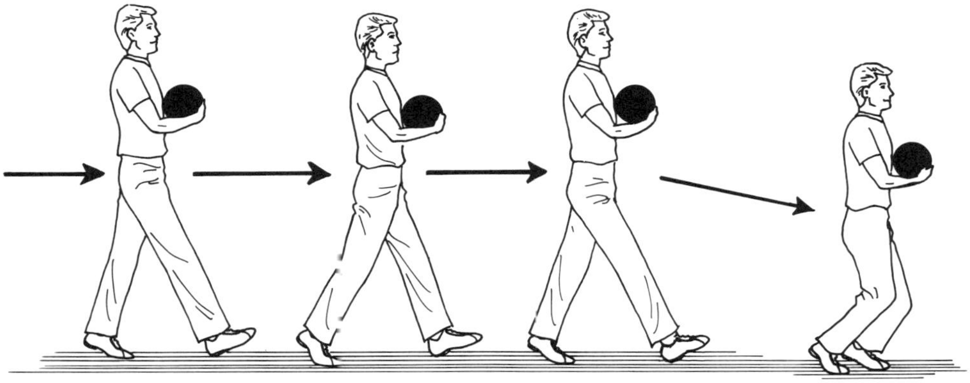

ERROR	CORRECTION
5. The bowler "sits" too soon during the footwork.	5. Check that the swingside leg does not start bending until after count "three" when the sliding foot pushes toward the foul line (see Drill 2).
Move to a position directly behind the student to check for Errors 6 and 7.	
6. The student walks too wide a track, too narrow a track, or in a cross-stepping pattern. The head moves from side to side.	6. Have student visualize the feet tracing a path slightly inside each hip and parallel with the swing.
7. The student is off balance at the foul line (a fallaway).	7. Have student keep his or her back straight, bend the swingside knee deeply, and push toward the line on count "four" (see Drill 1).

Footwork Drills

1. *Power Push*

[Corresponds to *Bowling*, Step 3, Drill 1]

Group Management and Safety Tips

- This is an individual drill.
- Let students alternate being on the approach after six trials.

Instructions to Class

- "Take a position about 4 feet from the foul line on the approach. Stand with both feet together. Do not put your fingers in the ball or align it with your swing plane. Hold the ball in both hands at waist-level and at the midline of your body."
- "Begin counting in groups of four to establish your cadence. To sharpen your sense of timing, subdivide your four-count cadence by adding an 'AND' between counts. Focus your eyes on the second arrow. On the 'AND' between 'three' and 'four,' begin stepping on your sliding foot."
- "On 'four' push your sliding foot toward the foul line. At the same time, bend your swingside leg, using it as an anchor."
- "On the 'AND' after 'four,' finish your slide by keeping your upper body straight and directly over your hips. Notice the feeling of stability and sitting tall, while holding this final slide position."

Student Option

- "You can make a game out of attaining the Success Goal. Ask a partner to rate your power push according to the characteristics in your book that are directly observed, not only felt. You both must agree upon selected rules."

Student Success Goal

- 8 out of 12 possible points

To Decrease Difficulty

- Allow use of a lighter ball.

To Increase Difficulty

- Increase the Success Goal to 10 of 12.

2. *Full Footwork and Cadence*

[Corresponds to *Bowling*, Step 3, Drill 2]

Group Management and Safety Tip

- This is a solo drill. Have students alternate being on a lane after every five attempts.

Instructions to Class

- "Take a midline ball setup at your normal setup location."
- "Begin counting your cadence as you did in Drill 1."
- "On the 'AND' after 'four,' step out with your swingside foot. On numbers 'two' and 'three,' take normal, heel-toe steps."
- "Do not place one foot in front of the other as in walking a straight line, do not step wider than your shoulders side-to-side, and do not cross one foot in front of the other. Keep your feet parallel and approximately three inches apart."
- "On 'four,' push your sliding foot forward, using your swingside foot as the anchor on the approach, thus incorporating the power push."
- "Notice that although each step occurs precisely on the numbered counts of your cadence, your motions should flow together. You should not hesitate between steps. Also remember that the time between steps is the same; the third and fourth steps are taken no faster than the first and second."

Student Option

- "Work with a partner, alternately rating each other using characteristics listed in your book."

Student Success Goal

- 10 out of 15 possible points

To Decrease Difficulty

- Allow use of a lighter ball.

To Increase Difficulty

- Not applicable.

3. *Starting Position Check*

[Corresponds to *Bowling*, Step 3, Drill 3]

Group Management and Safety Tips

- This is a solo drill. Have students alternate being on a lane after every five or ten attempts.
- Do not let students cross the foul line.
- Stress that students do not step on the object used as a marker on the approach, as they might slip.
- Paper markers, one with each student's name, represent a novel way of taking attendance.

Equipment

- Various small objects to mark desired sliding toe position (2 to 4 inches from foul line)—rulers, paper shapes, or pencils placed to the side.

Instructions to Class

- ''After practicing the previous drills, you are now ready to make a precise determination of how far from the foul line you should start your approach.''
- ''The conventional method has been to pace off four normal walking steps and add a half-step for the slide. This method is actually *undesirable* because it does not allow enough room for a sufficiently long push and slide.''
- ''Do the previous drill again. Start from your normal setup position. This time note how far your sliding toe stops from the foul line. Is it within the desired 2- to 4-inch range from the foul line?''
- ''Continue to adjust your starting position until you find the spot that allows your sliding toe to stop within 2 to 4 inches of the foul line. Now you have found your permanent setup starting position.''
- ''Repeat the previous drill 10 times, using your personalized starting position. Give yourself credit for each well-executed footwork drill in which you stop within the desired range.''

Student Option

- ''You may work with a partner.''

Student Success Goal

- 8 out of 10 well-executed, well-spaced footwork patterns

To Decrease Difficulty

- Reduce Success Goal to 6 of 10 footwork patterns.

To Increase Difficulty

- Increase Success Goal to 9 of 10 footwork patterns.

Step 4 Utility Delivery

The basic delivery described in this step is a framework upon which to build the techniques that your students will refine and polish in later steps. Hence, the name *utility delivery*. For the rest of this book, have your students incorporate the specific ball dynamics, strike targeting, and delivery refinements into this utility delivery. Such a strategy not only helps your students learn faster through structured experimentation but also satisfies the students' desire to roll the ball. Again, most details of the full delivery have been purposefully omitted to create the utility delivery, but the utility delivery will be progressively refined in subsequent steps until a coordinated finished delivery is achieved (Step 13).

Make sure to demonstrate how to execute the utility delivery, using the Student Keys to Success as a guide, until each student is performing adequately. Do not expect perfection from every student; the skills will improve with practice and refinement.

STUDENT KEYS TO SUCCESS

- Normal setup
- Count cadence
- Push ball and step forward before count ''one ''
- Elbows straight and swingside heel down on ''one''
- Let ball fall
- Ball low and sliding heel down on ''two''
- Ball high and swingside heel down on ''three''
- Ball low and sliding sole down on ''four''
- Back upright
- Release ball
- Follow through

Utility Delivery Drill

Utility Delivery

[Corresponds to *Bowling*, Step 4 Drill]

Group Management and Safety Tips

- Demonstrate for the entire group. Direct the students in a run-through without balls. The students should set up side by side on adjacent lanes. They should move together as a class to the foul line, executing the utility delivery as proficiently as possible.
- You may have them do a ''stop-action'' delivery first. Point out the ball and foot positions as your students stand frozen in each delivery position. Then you may have them build up to a flowing motion at game speed.
- Here are the proper ball and foot positions:

Count	Ball position	Foot in front
1	Straight out in front of shoulder	Swingside (heel down)
2	Straight down	Balance side (heel down)
3	Straight out in back of shoulder	Swingside (heel down
4 (slide)	Straight down	Balance side (toe down)

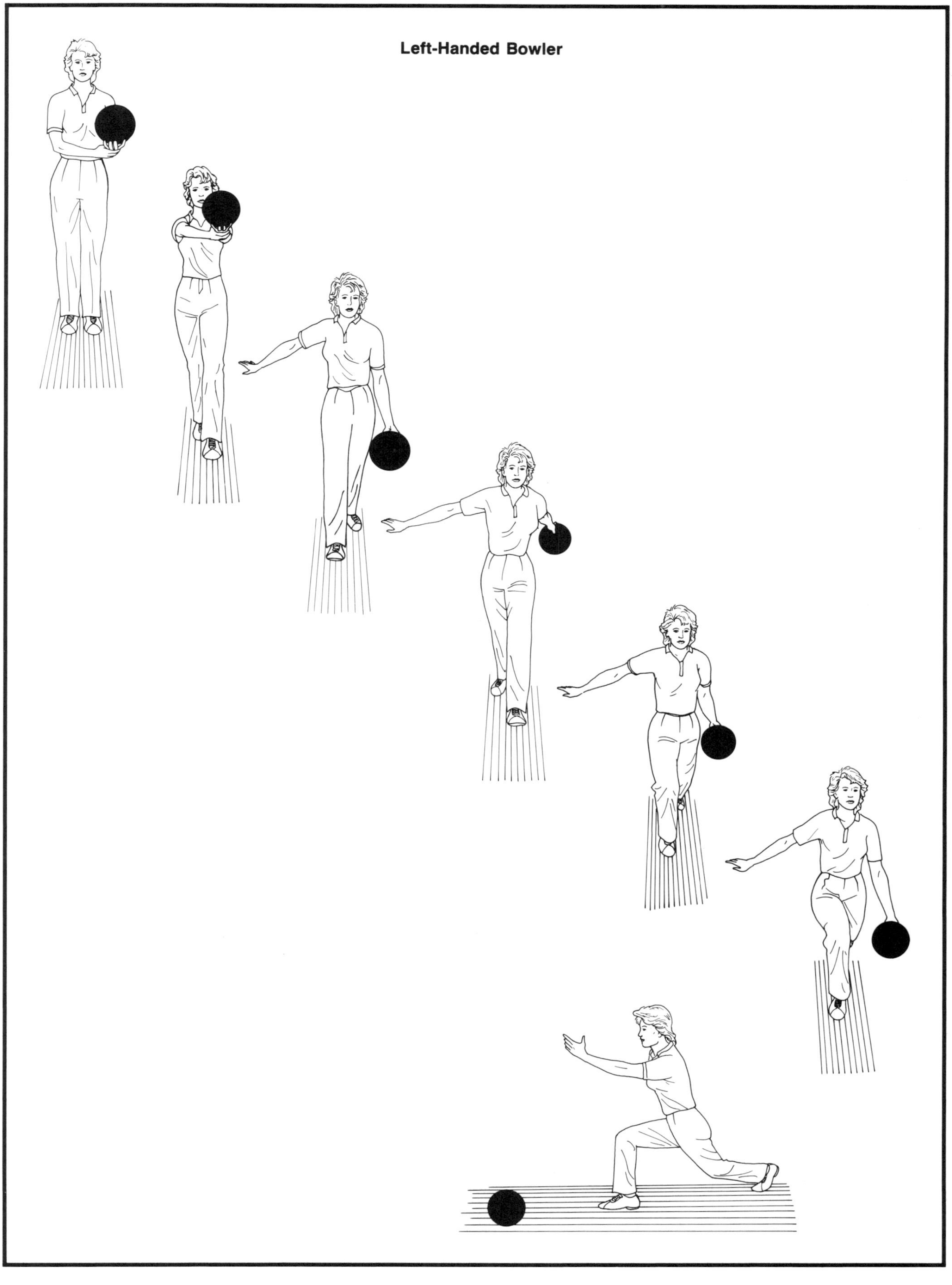
Left-Handed Bowler

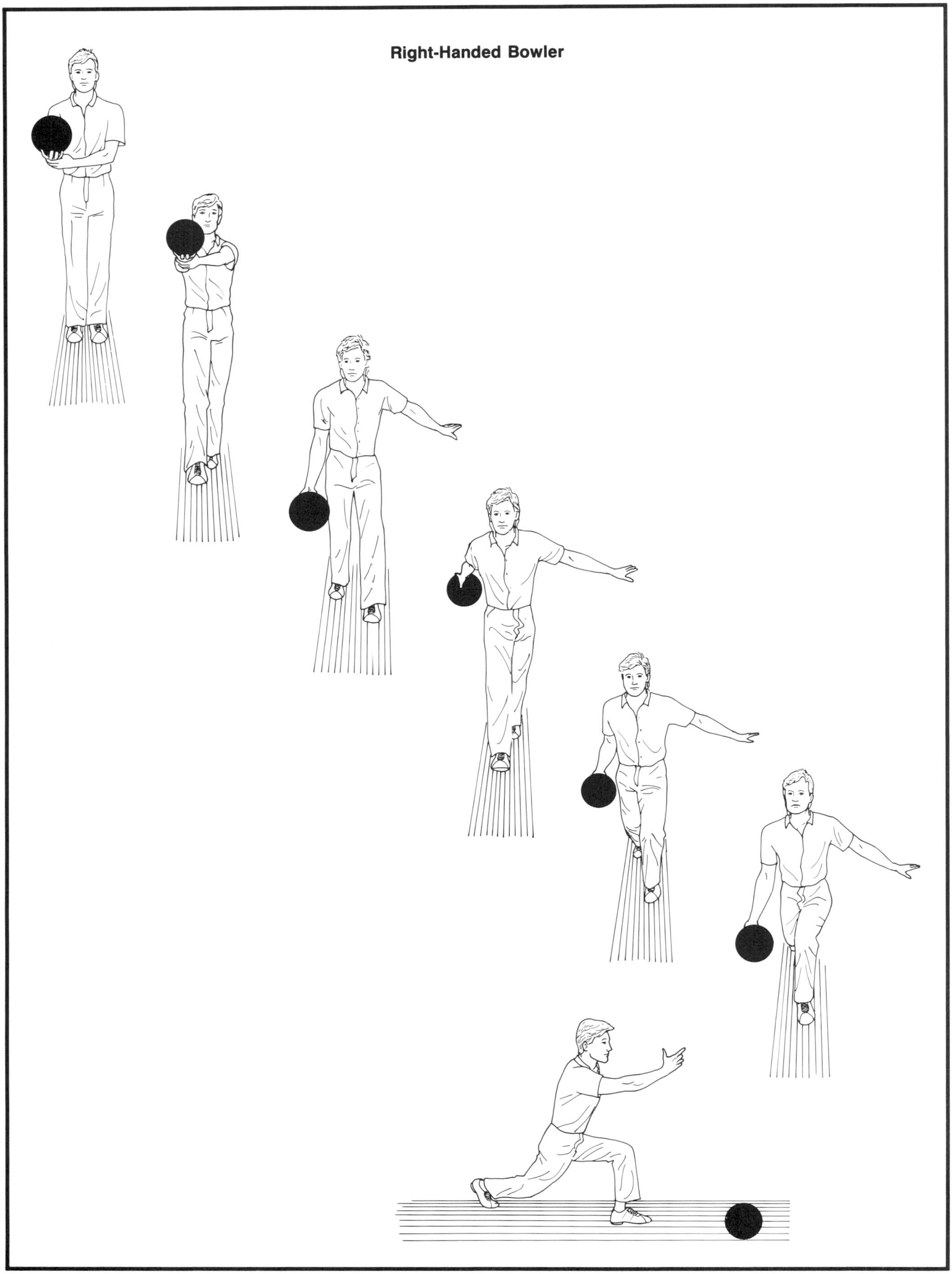

Instructions to Class

- "Assume your proper setup position. Begin counting your cadence."
- "Halfway between count 'four' and the next 'one,' push your ball forward with both hands, directly in line with your bowling shoulder. At the same time, begin stepping forward with your swingside foot so that both arms become straight and your swingside heel touches down on count 'one.'"
- "When both arms are straight out and your swingside heel touches the floor, let your ball swing freely; keep walking, taking two more steps and a slide."
- "Remember to match your footwork to your pendulum swing—not the reverse."

Student Option

- "With a partner, select how many utility deliveries to make before alternating."

Student Success Goal

- 20 utility deliveries

To Decrease Difficulty

- Let the student run through the drill without the ball, then build to game speed with a ball.
- Have student stand beside either you or an accomplished bowling partner and mirror coordination.

To Increase Difficulty

- Have student compare the feeling of balance with a utility delivery taken from a setup both with and without a sufficient amount of space (3 inches) between feet.

Step 5 Ball Dynamics

Your students need to develop the ability to actively use the collective *skidding* and *rolling* motions of a bowling ball to knock down the pins most effectively. These ball *dynamics* are popularly called ''ball reaction.''

Two reaction types, the straight ball and the hook ball, are emphasized because (a) straight-ball skills lead to those of the hook ball, and (b) both types are useful in certain cases. The properly executed straight ball proceeds along a path from the hand, over the target point, and straight to the desired point of impact at the pins. It should not veer to the outside (backup) or to the inside (hook). The properly executed hook ball proceeds along a straight path from the hand, over the target point, and down the lane. At the break point, approximately two-thirds to three-quarters of the way down the lane, it should veer, or hook, toward the inside of the lane and continue to the desired point of impact with the object pins. Other types of ball dynamics, the backup ball and the curve ball, are mentioned but not explained in detail because they are poor alternatives to the hook ball and are not recommended (see Figure 5.1).

Effective ball dynamics take a fairly long time to master. However, there are certain biomechanical principles that lead to effective ball dynamics:

1. The greatest mechanical efficiency is obtained if the swing plane is aligned with the desired target.
2. More force can be applied in the desired direction of the ball if the hand is kept in a position more behind the ball, and if the stroke is finished with a strong follow-through.
3. Using the back foot to push against the approach at the instant of release helps give more accurate projection toward the target as well as more rotation. Naturally, a secure grip and a firm, straight wrist facilitate transfer of momentum from the body to the ball.

Throughout the descriptions, note that the clockface terminology used for hand positions refers to the direction in which the *tips* of the bowling fingers (not the thumb) are pointing with the palm perpendicular to the target line for straight-ball deliveries or with the palm at a 45 degree angle to the target line for hook-ball deliveries.

STUDENT KEYS TO SUCCESS

- Stable at start
- Correct hand position
- Hand position maintained

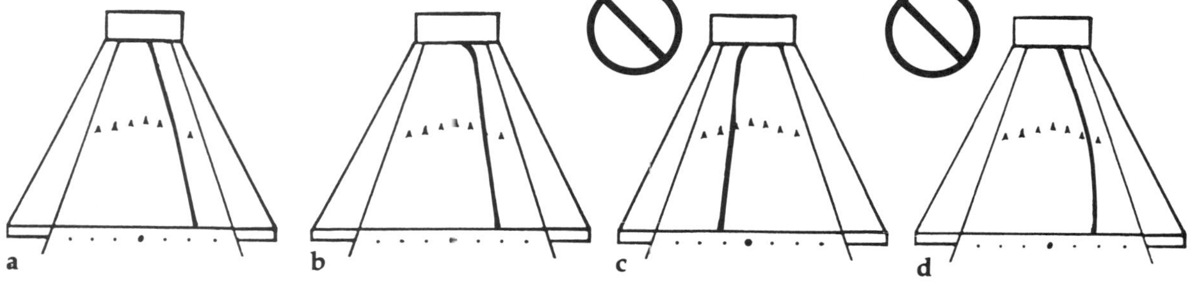

Figure 5.1 The (a) straight- and (b) hook-ball reactions are recommended but the (c) backup and (d) curve reactions are not (right-handed examples).

Ball Dynamics Rating		
CRITERION	**BEGINNING LEVEL**	**ACCOMPLISHED LEVEL**
Preparation	• Hand not in correct position	• Wrist firm • For straight-ball delivery: fingers at 12 o'clock, like an underhand roll • For hook-ball delivery: fingers at 10 o'clock (right-handed bowler) or 2 o'clock (left-handed bowler): fingers positioned between an underhand roll and a handshake
Execution and Recovery	• Hand position changes erratically	• Hand maintains firm, proper position

Error Detection and Correction for Ball Dynamics

Errors in ball dynamics usually result from an improper hand position at the release and a misaligned swing. Also, timing errors, such as early and late balls, often cause errors in the path of a hook ball. All of the following errors refer to the reaction of the ball as it proceeds down the lane toward the pins.

To observe the typical errors in the way your students' balls roll down the lanes, take a position behind and slightly to the swingside of the student. Gaze first at the foul line; as soon as the ball touches down, follow it with your eyes. Get into the habit of observing the motion of the ball this way.

ERROR	**CORRECTION**
For Straight Ball	
1. Ball veers off to one side of the lane instead of going straight along the desired path.	1. Tell your student to hold fingers at 12 o'clock with a firm wrist, and with the palm perpendicular to the swing plane.

ERROR	CORRECTION
2. Ball seems to be sliding instead of rolling.	2. Restate the importance of a firm wrist. Tell your student to attend to the feel of the pendulum swing and the release. If the ball seems to catch on the student's thumb, or "hang," then check the student's ball fit.
3. Ball is rolling over the grip holes, creating a "flat tire" sound.	3. Warn the student not to rotate the wrist at the point of release. Have the student correct the finger position, check for wrist firmness, and check the ball fit. Remind the student to keep the elbow straight.
For Hook Ball	
1. Ball misses either the visual target, the desired point of impact with the pins, or both.	1. Have the student make sure that the fingers are not too far toward the inside (8 or 9 o'clock for a right-handed bowler; 3 or 4 o'clock for a left-handed bowler). This would allow the arm to move too far away from the body, making the ball touch down too far to the outside. Check the student's execution of the delivery again.
2. Ball hooks too little.	2. Tell the student to keep a firm wrist. Check that the fingers are in the proper position. Make sure that the student feels good leverage at the release. If you notice a hanging thumb, check the student's ball fit.
3. Ball hooks too much.	3. Have your student keep the wrist firm and the fingers in the proper position. Check to see whether the student is rolling the ball with normal speed. Check for a hanging thumb.
4. Ball hooks inconsistently.	4. Tell the student to keep the wrist firm and the fingers in the proper position, and to roll the ball at the same speed every time.
5. Ball rolls over the grip holes, creating a "flat tire" sound.	5. Check and correct the student's finger position, wrist firmness, and ball fit. Remind the student to keep the elbow straight and not to rotate the wrist to the inside or outside at the release.

Ball Dynamics Drills

1. High-Leverage Straight-Ball Finish

[Corresponds to *Bowling,* Step 5, Drill 1]

Group Management and Safety Tips

- One person at a time per lane.
- Because the straight-ball hand position places the lifting fingers closer to the sliding foot, this drill can be used to evaluate the developing finger leverage as the timing between swing and slide improves.
- If any student has extreme difficulty in keeping the wrist straight, a wrist brace may be beneficial.

Instructions to Class

- ''Assume a setup position 4 feet from the foul line, with your gripping fingers (middle and index) at the 12 o'clock position.''
- 'Begin your cadence, focus on your visual target, take a one-step delivery by combining the pendulum swing, the power push (Step 3, Drill 1), and rolling the ball.''
- ''Do not begin your power push until the ball is at the top of the backswing at count 'three.' ''
- ''You should feel more pressure on your lifting fingers, and you should feel your bowling shoulder supporting your straight bowling arm. These two kinesthetic sensations are termed 'fingers in the shot' and 'shoulder in the shot' respectively.''

Student Options

- ''With a partner, decide on an order of rotation.''
- ''After 12 one-step deliveries, decide how many more 'repetitions you need to feel a stable one-step delivery.''

Student Success Goal

- 18 one-step straight-ball deliveries

To Decrease Difficulty

- Reduce the Success Goal.

To Increase Difficulty

- Increase the Success Goal.

2. *Full Straight-Ball Delivery*

[Corresponds to *Bowling*, Step 5, Drill 2]

Group Management and Safety Tip

- One person at a time per lane.

Instructions to Class

- "Assume a normal setup position."
- "Roll the ball using a smooth, flowing, full straight-ball delivery."
- "End with the high-leverage lift, finish, and follow-through you practiced in the last drill."

Student Options

- "Prior to evaluating your deliveries, select between 5 to 10 repetitions to practice at your own pace."
- "Ask a partner to evaluate your deliveries."

Student Success Goal

- 24 full straight-ball deliveries

To Decrease Difficulty

- Reduce the Success Goal.

To Increase Difficulty

- Increase the Success Goal.

3. *Hook-Ball Finish*

[Corresponds to *Bowling*, Step 5, Drill 3]

Group Management and Safety Tip

- One person at a time per lane.

Instructions to Class

- "Assume a setup position 4 feet from the foul line. Move your gripping fingers 45 degrees to the inside of the 12 o'clock position."
- "Begin your cadence, focus on your visual target, take a one-step delivery like Drill 1, but roll a hook ball."
- "The hook is accomplished by imparting lift in a direction not in line with the ball's path so that the ball will skid farther down the lane (approximately 15 feet), roll approximately 30 feet, and then hook within 15 feet of the pins."

Student Options

- "With a partner, decide on a rotation order."
- "After 12 one-step deliveries, decide how many more repetitions you need to feel a consistent release."

Student Success Goal

- 18 one-step hook-ball deliveries

To Decrease Difficulty

- Reduce the Success Goal.

To Increase Difficulty

- Increase the Success Goal.

4. *Full Hook-Ball Delivery*

[Corresponds to *Bowling*, Step 5, Drill 4]

Group Management and Safety Tip

- One person at a time per lane.

Instructions to Class

- "Assume a normal setup position with your fingers 45 degrees to the inside of the 12 o'clock position as in the previous drill."
- "Roll the ball using a smooth, flowing, full hook-ball delivery."
- "Again, notice that the hook is accomplished by imparting lift in a direction not in line with the ball's path so that the ball will skid farther down the lane (approximately 15 feet), roll approximately 30 feet, and then hook within 15 feet of the pins."

Student Options

- "Prior to evaluating your deliveries, select between 5 to 10 repetitions to practice at your own pace."
- "Ask a partner to evaluate your deliveries."

Student Success Goal

- 24 full hook-ball deliveries

To Decrease Difficulty

- Reduce the Success Goal.

To Increase Difficulty

- Increase the Success Goal.

5. *Marked Axis Dynamics Awareness*

[Corresponds to *Bowling*, Step 5, Drill 5]

Group Management and Safety Tips

- Two students per lane work together.
- Allow the use of tape only during practice; it is not allowed in sanctioned leagues or tournament play.

Equipment

- White or yellow wax pencils, 1 per student pair
- Brightly colored plastic tape, 1-inch roll
- Scissors
- Wiping cloths, 1 per student pair

Instructions to Class

- "Before you roll a ball, wipe it off very well. Then deliver the ball once in your normal delivery. Find the ring of oil, or lane dressing, on the surface of the ball; this is your ball track."
- "Lightly mark this track with a wax pencil."
- "Find the 'center' of the circle formed by the track. This center is the negative axis pole, the axis pole that you cannot see as the ball rolls down the lane."

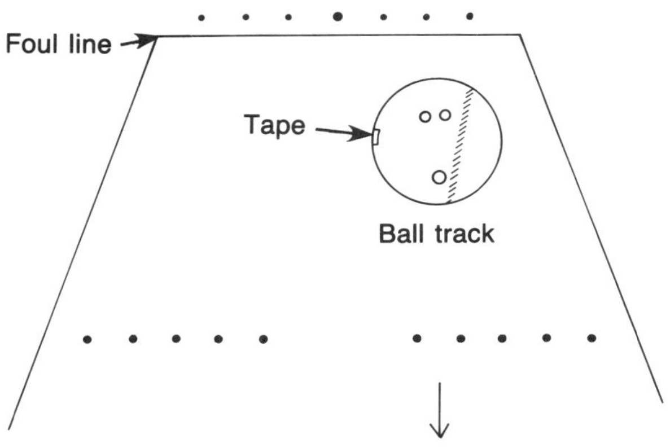

Left-Handed Bowler

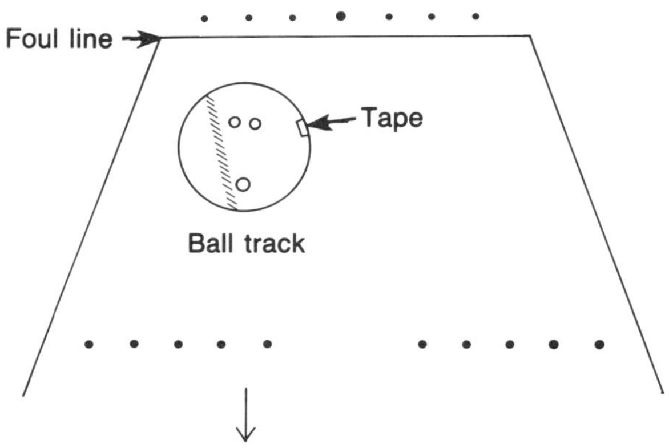

Right-Handed Bowler

- ''Next, imagine a line extending from the negative axis pole directly through the center of the ball to the opposite side. The axis pole directed toward the headpin as the ball rolls down the lane is the positive axis pole. You can see this axis pole as the ball rolls down the lane.''
- ''Mark the positive axis pole by putting a 1-inch square of brightly colored plastic tape on it. The tape should contrast with the ball's color so you can easily see it. Wipe the wax pencil marks off of your ball before you begin to bowl again.''
- ''Roll your ball consistently down the lane. Reposition the tape after each shot until the tape appears motionless (not wobbling) as your ball rolls down the lane, indicating that the tape is perfectly positioned over the center of the positive axis pole, the pole you can see. The tape will wobble more when you use the hook ball.''

Student Options

- ''Ask a partner to evaluate your straight-ball and hook-ball deliveries according to the Keys to Success Checklist in your book.''
- ''Create a game with your partner to see who can consistently keep the tape on the marked axis from wobbling. Mutually agree upon the rules for your game.''

Student Success Goal

- Alternate 10 straight balls with 10 hook balls

To Decrease Difficulty

- Reduce the Success Goal.

To Increase Difficulty

- Increase the Success Goal.
- Have student alternate 2 straight balls with 2 hook balls to reach the Success Goal.

Step 6 Strike Targeting

Now your students are ready to apply what they have learned about straight and hook balls to making strikes. Strike bowling is easy; it is simply making accurate shots toward intelligently selected targets on the lane. A lane target is some mark—a dark spot in a board, a crack between boards, an arrow, or a dot—used for aiming. A strike *targeting system* is an orderly plan by which a bowler uses targets, even before rolling the ball, to maximize the chance of a strike. The most difficult aspect of targeting is keeping the gaze fixed on the target until the ball has passed it.

Straight-ball strike targeting is introduced first to provide feedback and avoid the inherent problems of the hook. Hook-ball strike-targeting skills are then added.

An effective targeting system uses two points of reference for the ball path—one at the foul line and one at the level of the arrows on the lane—connected by a *target line*. This target line requires an *approach line* upon which to walk during the delivery. Stress to your students that no targeting system should ever require that the swing or gait be changed to accommodate poorly considered lane targets.

Four different aiming methods are mentioned in the participant's book: pin bowling, spot bowling, line bowling, and target-line or parallel-line bowling. However, only target-line bowling—the only true targeting system—is described in detail. Focusing on a point yields a biomechanical advantage to improve balance: A visual fixation point (visual target) correctly in line with the target line stabilizes the head in the proper spatial relationship with the target, luring the body more consistently in line with the target during the delivery.

A strike-targeting system is useful to your students for the following reasons:

1. Accuracy is increased by using closer targets versus the pins as the visual fixation point.
2. Shot to shot consistency is increased.
3. With a hook ball, it is easier to locate the best path for your ball to follow.
4. It is easier to be more responsive to changing lane conditions.

Strike targeting effectiveness cannot be mastered within a single course; the skills take months—even years—to develop. Consequently, your students will show a very wide range of targeting abilities. You should practice watching bowlers deliver the ball, paying close attention to the ball path.

STUDENT KEYS TO SUCCESS

- Choose target point
- Choose touchdown point
- Take appropriate setup location
- Feet parallel with target line
- Focus eyes on visual target
- Execute well
- Analyze results
- Adjust target line
- Repeat execution

Strike Targeting Rating

CRITERION	BEGINNING LEVEL	ACCOMPLISHED LEVEL
Target Line	• No concept	• Clear choice, for example, straight ball, 8-to-10, or hook ball, 10-to-10
Setup Location	• No concept	• Appropriate for chosen target line
Angle of Feet to Target Line	• No concept	• Feet parallel with the target line and approach line
Visual Target	• Looks at pins	• Proper visual target (second arrow)
Target-Line Adjustment	• No concept	• Appropriate in response to previous delivery

Error Detection and Correction for Strike Targeting

Take a position behind and slightly to the swingside of the student for all the following observations. Gaze first at the foul line to note on what board the ball touches down. After the ball touches down, follow it and note what board it crosses at the level of the arrows. Note also the board number over which the ball rolls as it hits the pins; board 17 is the strike pocket.

ERROR	CORRECTION
Straight Ball	
1. Ball misses the target to the inside and hits too high on the headpin, or completely misses the headpin to the inside.	1. Have your student make sure that the swing is in line with the shoulder and the target. Also make sure that the student is not looking to the inside of the target.

ERROR	CORRECTION
2. Ball misses the target to the outside and hits too light on the headpin, or completely misses the headpin to the outside.	2. Make sure the swing is in line with the shoulder and the target. Also make sure that the student is not looking to the outside of the target.
3. Ball consistently hits the target, but misses the point of impact at the pins by the same amount each time.	3. Check the alignment of the swing with the target. Have the student move the setup in the same direction as the impact error; if the ball is missing to the outside of the pocket, have the student move the setup location to the outside, and vice versa. The student may need to recompute the placement distance.
4. Ball consistently misses the target by the same amount each time.	4. Check the execution and the swing alignment. Ask the student to move his or her gaze in the direction opposite the error until the ball is rolling consistently over the target point (see Drill 4).
5. Ball consistently hits the target and the strike pocket, but does not strike.	5. Make half-board adjustments in your student's setup location until the ball is hitting the pocket in the proper way to carry the pins.
Hook Ball	
1. Ball hits the target point but misses the strike pocket to the inside, hitting the headpin too full, or missing it altogether to the inside.	1. Instruct your student to try again with proper execution and the correct visual target. If the second attempt does not work, move the student to a more inside setup location, 2 boards at a time, until the ball hits the strike pocket.
2. Ball hits the target point but misses the strike pocket to the outside, hitting the headpin too lightly, or missing it altogether to the outside.	2. Instruct your student to try again using proper execution and the correct visual target. If the second attempt does not work, move the student's setup location more outside, 2 boards at a time, until the ball hits the strike pocket.
3. Ball consistently misses the target point.	3. Use Drill 4 to help student problem-solve corrections.

ERROR	CORRECTION
4. Ball consistently hits the target and the strike pocket, but does not strike consistently.	4. Check the swing for alignment with the shoulder and the target. Help your student make slight adjustments in finger position (e.g., to change from the 45-degree to a 30- or 60-degree position) to create a different ball reaction. Tell the student that he or she may have to move the setup location in response to the different amount of hook. If the hook is bigger, the feet should be moved to the inside; if smaller, to the outside.

Strike-Targeting Drills

1. *Placement Distance Determination*

[Corresponds to *Bowling*, Step 6, Drill 2]

Group Management and Safety Tips

- Two students work together per lane.
- Partner needs to stay on either side of bowler at the foul line.

Equipment

- 12-inch rulers, 1 per student pair

Instructions to Class

- ''Take a delivery position at the foul line with your ball dangling to your swingside.''
- ''Then 'sit' even lower than normal until the ball touches the approach. Maintain proper posture.''
- ''Partners use a ruler to measure the distance between the inner edge of the sliding foot and the center of the ball touching the approach. Repeat five times.''
- ''Average the five measurements and you have your own placement distance in inches. Divide this figure by 1.1 to get your placement distance (PD) in boards.''

Student Option

- None

Student Success Goal

- Determine personal PD in boards after 5 measurements

To Decrease Difficulty

- Not applicable.

To Increase Difficulty

- Not applicable.

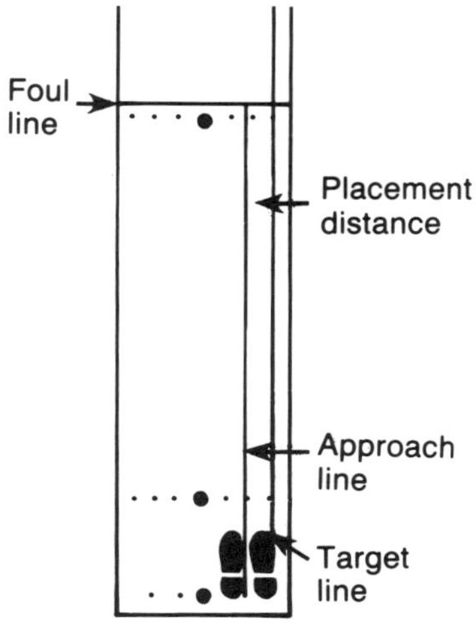

2. *Straight-Ball Strike Targeting*

[Corresponds to *Bowling*, Step 6, Drill 3]

Group Management and Safety Tips

- Two students per lane: One bowls while the other observes and records.
- During this drill, let student talk to partner as directed, but discourage visiting.

Equipment

- 1 roll of dark tape, optional

Instructions to Class

- "Now you are going to bowl 10 first-ball deliveries using an 8-to-10 target line."
- "Partners, you will be recording information but not the number of pins knocked down. Prepare your scoresheet following the example shown in Sample Scoresheet 1 in your book."
- "Bowlers, set up on the same board every time. Be sure to tell your partner what board this is because it will be recorded as your 'setup' location. After you roll the ball, look at your sliding toe. The first *whole* board to the inside of that foot is your 'slide location.' After each ball, tell your partner what board it is."
- "Partners, your job is to watch for and record the board over which the ball passed when it passed the arrows (target area board), and the board over which it rolled when it hit the pins (impact board). Don't watch the bowler's form. Give the bowler a point whenever an entry matches the ideal location as described in your book."
- "Bowlers, after the 10 balls, discuss your performance with your partner, using the characteristics listed in your book."

Student Option

- "Decide rotation order with your partner."

Student Success Goal

- Complete 3 trial games, rating slide location, target area, impact board, and total points

To Decrease Difficulty

- Ask student to correctly answer the Targeting Quiz (Step 6, Drill 1) in the participant's book.
- Reduce the Success Goal.
- Move the target closer by putting a piece of dark tape on the target area board. Use 2-foot increments until student is regularly hitting target area board.

To Increase Difficulty

- Increase the Success Goal.

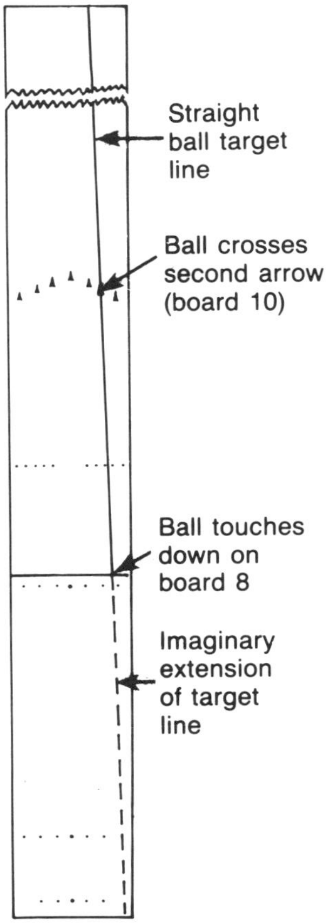

3. *Hook-Ball Strike Targeting*

[Corresponds to *Bowling*, Step 6, Drill 4]

Group Management and Safety Tip

- Two students work per lane, one bowling while the other observes and records.

Equipment

- 1 roll of dark tape, optional

Instructions to Class

- "In this drill, you bowl a trial game of 10 first balls. Warm up using a 10-to-10 target line. Also, start the game with a 10-to-10 target line."
- "Partners, prepare a scoresheet as shown in Sample Scoresheet 2 in your book."
- "Bowlers, before each first ball, tell your partner your intended target line."
- "Partners, record the intended line and whether or not the bowler hit it. After the bowler successfully hits the intended target, record the number of the board over which the ball rolled when it hit the pins."
- "Bowlers, you may have to make several first-ball attempts each frame before you hit your intended target line."
- "Repeat the above procedures moving your setup location as explained in Hook Ball Corrections 1 and 2, until you find your proper target line for hitting the pocket."

Student Option

- "Select between 2 and 4 warm-up trials to practice at your own pace."

Student Success Goal

- 4 pocket hits in a row within a single trial game, or completion of 3 trial games

To Decrease Difficulty

- Ask student to correctly answer the Targeting Quiz (Step 6, Drill 1) in the participant's book.
- Reduce the Success Goal.
- Move the target closer by putting a piece of dark tape on the target area board closer to the bowler, using 2-foot increments.

To Increase Difficulty

- Increase the Success Goal.

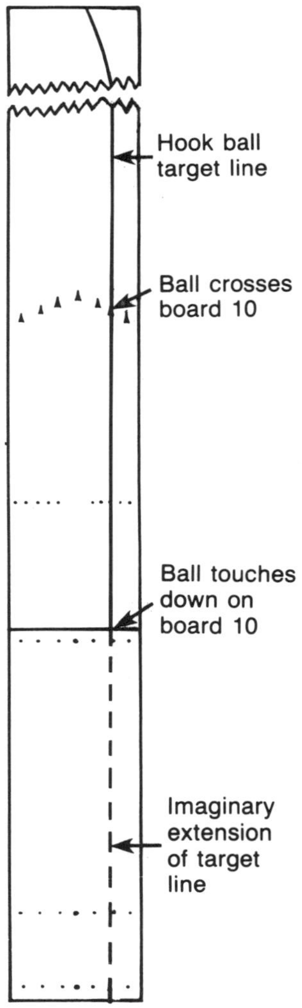

4. *Correcting Visual Targeting Error*

[New drill]

Group Management and Safety Tips

- This is an optional instructor's discretionary drill appropriate for a student who consistently misses his or her visual target.
- *Rationale*: It is sometimes necessary to reorient a student's thinking regarding the visual target and the target point. The visual target is simply a point on the lane to fix the gaze on, one that draws the body in such a direction as to make the ball roll over a desired target point.

For example, if a student wishes to roll the ball along a 10-to-10 target line, the 10th board being the touchdown point at the foul line and the 10th board (second arrow) being the target point at the arrows, it would be convenient for the student to use the second arrow as the visual target.

Although occasionally possible, such is often not the case. Because the head is not positioned directly over the bowling arm, because of excessive arm splay (see Step

8, Drill 4), or because of some other visual problem, a student may have to fix the gaze to the side of the target point. Consequently, it will benefit the student to (a) realize the disparity between the two targets, (b) determine the proper place to look in relation to a desired target point, and (c) consistently apply the compensation in all future bowling activity. You can use this drill to help your student accomplish the first two of these three objectives.

- *Procedure*: First approach your student and ask what target line and visual target is being used. Then instruct your student to roll several shots along this target line, using the same visual target. Also instruct your student to inform you, upon returning from the foul line, of the location where the ball crossed at the level of the arrows. Compare your student's response with your actual observation.

  If your student says that the ball rolled over the visual target (where the student was looking, or spotting), and it actually did, no adjustment in the visual target is necessary.

  If your student says that the ball rolled over the visual target, but it actually did not, some adjustment in the visual target is necessary.

  Help your student problem-solve (by trial and error, if necessary) to look (to the inside or the outside) for the ball to roll over the selected visual target point.

Instructions to Individual

- "You may have a visual error that must be compensated for if there is a consistent difference between your visual target—the place where you look—and your target point—the place where you want your ball to cross at the level of the arrows."
- "First, answer these questions:

  What target line are you using?

  What do you look at when attempting to use this target line?

  Where do you stand in the setup for this target?"
- "Then, roll several shots using this target line and your usual visual target. After you return from the foul line, identify what board your ball rolled over at the level of the arrows."
- "Did you execute properly?" [If the answer is no, disregard the attempt and instruct your student to roll another ball. If the answer is yes, continue.]
- "Over what board did you see your ball roll?" [Compare the student's response with your observation. Make a written note if necessary, but do not inform your student of your observation until all trials have been completed. Instruct your student to roll another ball, if necessary. Discontinue trials if you have determined a consistent difference.]
- "Now slightly adjust your visual target (to the inside or outside) so that your ball is actually consistently rolling over the desired target point." [Begin the trial-and-error adjustment. Instruct the student to move the gaze in the direction opposite the miss—if the ball misses the target point to the inside, the gaze must be moved the same amount to the outside—until the ball is rolling consistently over the target point. Always check for quality of execution. If the student does not execute properly, regardless of outcome at the level of the arrows, always say, "Ok, now let's make another shot and concentrate on executing well this time."]

Student Option

- "Select the total number of deliveries you want to practice at your own pace."

Student Success Goal

- 10 attempts at rolling the ball accurately over a desired point using the adjusted visual target

To Decrease Difficulty

- Ask student to correctly answer Targeting Quiz (Step 6, Drill 1) in the participant's book.

To Increase Difficulty

- Not applicable.

5. Curtain Bowling

[New drill]

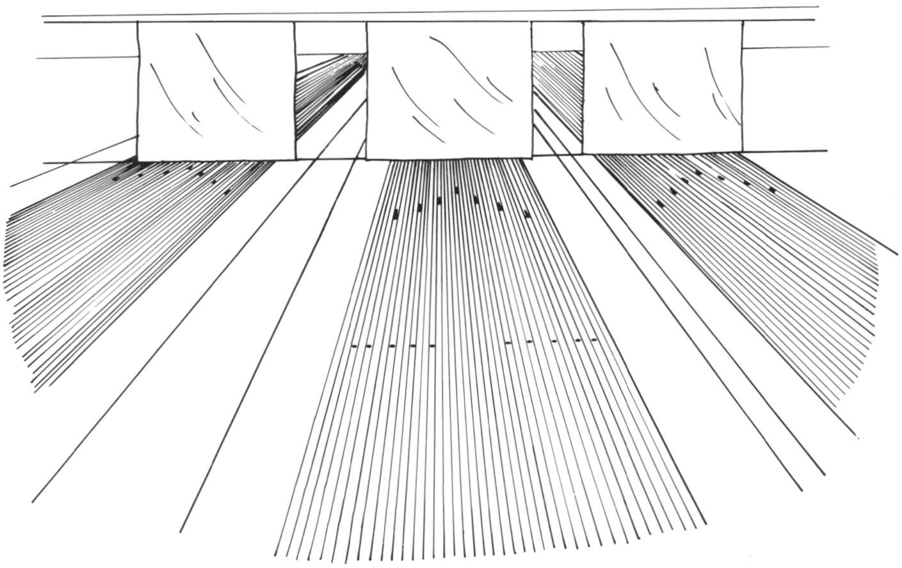

Group Management and Safety Tips

- This optional, advanced drill refines strike-targeting and can be used for beginning a spare-targeting system.
- The technique involves bowling 2 regulation game lines with a 4-foot-square curtain hanging directly over the wooden part of the lane. Its bottom edge is approximately 10 inches over the lane surface at a point 2 feet past the arrows. The area above both channels is left open so the bowler can see the pins, when necessary.
- You should prepare the lanes by stringing two lines across the bowling center, one 10 inches above the lane surface and the other 4 feet 10 inches above the surface. Use clothespins to secure both the tops and the bottoms of the curtains (which are made of lightweight material such as muslin or percale) to the lines. If possible, leave an open space directly over the channels so that students can see which pins were knocked down for scoring purposes.

Equipment

- Clotheslines, lengths depending on number of lanes
- Clothespins, 4 or more per lane
- Lightweight (bed) sheets or bolts of lightweight cloth, amount depending on number of lanes

Instructions to Class

- "This drill will help you better use the targeting aids on the lane. Complete 2 regulation games, while using only the dots and arrows as targeting aids. You may look at the pins between shots to determine your score."
- "Because you have not yet been taught how to make spares using the targeting aids, just use the second arrow as your visual target. But, move your setup location in the opposite direction of the spare leave: If your spare is on the left side, move your body to the right; if the spare is on the right side, move your body to the left. Then, experiment with walking in the direction of the spare leave."

Student Options

- "Create your own scoring system with a partner."
- "With a partner, alternate taking the first versus the second roll."

Student Success Goal

- Complete 2 regulation games while using only the dots and arrows as targeting aids.

To Decrease Difficulty

- Reduce the Success Goal.
- Have student bowl only for targeting points.

To Increase Difficulty

- Have student bowl for a total score, counting both strikes and spares.

6. *Clothespin Target or Hurdles*

[New drill]

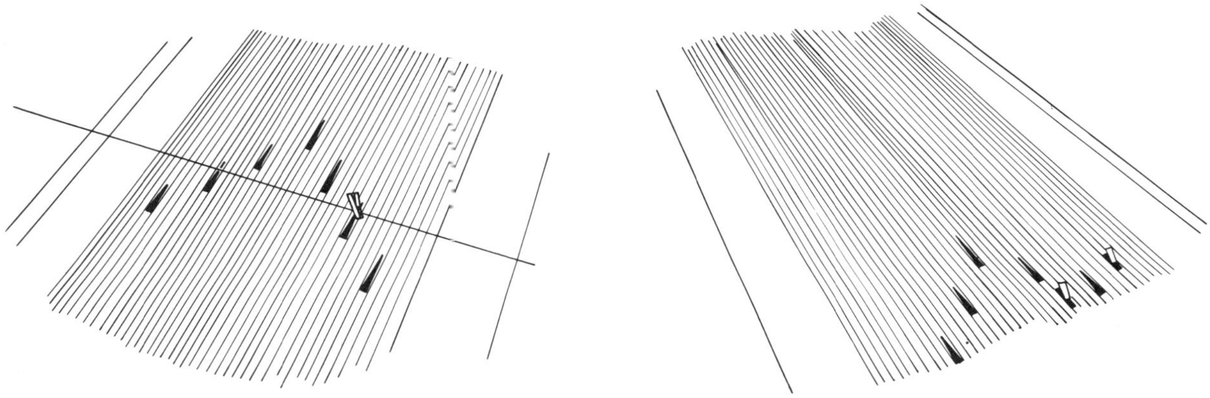

Group Management and Safety Tips

- This optional drill also refines the target-line system for strikes and spares.
- String one clothesline or heavy string across the bowling center, 10 inches above the lane surface. Clamp a clothespin on the line, directly over the second arrow, at a level such that the ball will touch the clothespin only if it rolls over the second arrow. Award 10 points for hitting the clothespin but do not deduct points for not hitting it.
- *Variation*: Be sure to coordinate this procedure with the proprietor of the establishment; use only approved cleaner. Clean the oil dressing off the section of the lane to which you will affix the tape.

For each lane, cut two pieces of posterboard 1 inch wide and approximately 5 inches long. Cut four pieces of 1-inch-wide plastic tape, each approximately 4 inches long. Affix two pieces of tape to both sides of the same end of each piece of posterboard, with about 2 inches of each piece of tape hanging over. Take care not to let the tape pieces stick to each other.

Next, stand up one piece of posterboard on Board 6 and another on Board 14, with the free ends of the tape down so that the posterboard is standing up. The back piece of tape should be pointed down the lane, toward the pins, while the front piece of tape should pop the posterboard back up if it is hit by the ball. The goal is to hit the target arrow, between the hurdles.

Equipment

- Clothesline or heavy string
- Clothespins, 1 per class
- Optional: cardboard or posterboard, scissors, and tape

Instructions to Class

- ''This drill will help you become more accurate. Please complete 2 regulation games, trying as best you can to hit your lane target every time. The objective is for you to roll the ball directly over your target, thereby making the ball touch the clothespin. Only balls right over the target will touch the clothespin.''
- ''If your ball touches the clothespin, add 10 points to your score, for a total of 20 possible points per frame.''
- ''Because you have not yet been taught how to make spares using the targeting aids, continue to use the second arrow as your visual target at all times. But, move your setup location in the direction opposite the spare leave: If your spare is on the left side, move your body to the right; if the spare is on the right side, move your body to the left. Just take a 'trial and error' approach at this time as you walk in the direction of the spare leave.''

Student Options

- ''Select the number of games to practice at your own pace, as well as with a partner.''
- ''In agreement with partners at the next lane, the winning partners bowl the next game together.''

Student Success Goal

- Complete 2 regulation games using the second arrow as your strike target

To Decrease Difficulty

- Add additional clothespins (1 or 2 board widths from target), and award points for hitting any clothespin.

To Increase Difficulty

- Complete 3 regulation games.

7. 3-0-1-2 Targeting System

[New drill]

Description of System

- This is an optional targeting system appropriate for advanced students with a desire for more information, if you have time to instruct them. It is based on ratios which reflect (a) the board numbers upon which the pins, approach dots, and lane targeting markers are placed and (b) the relative length of the lane segments, from the back of the approach to the headpin. A rule based on these ratios can be stated: For every 3 boards of change in the point of impact of the ball without changing the target point (or visual target) (0, or ''zero,'' change) used, one should change the position of the setup at the back of the approach 2 boards in the *opposite* direction from the point of impact. This will result in a 1-board difference at the foul line.

Imagine a 75-foot stick (representing your target line) held by a nail driven into your target arrow on the lane. This ''stick'' pivots at your visual target point. For example, if you are right handed, want to strike, and your impact point is left of the strike pocket, move your setup left or to your inside.

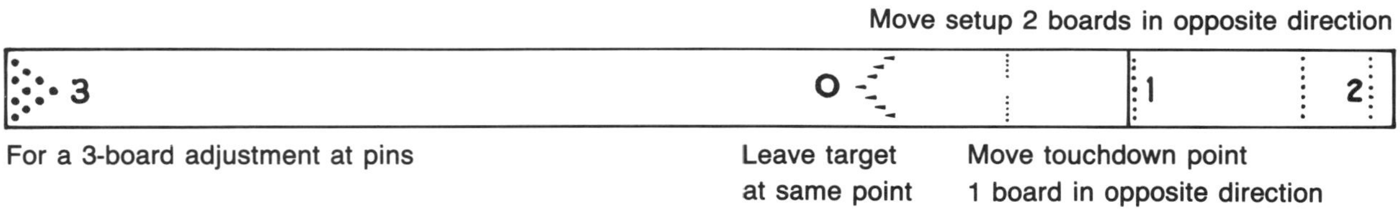

Adjusting for a Strike

- The "base number" to which all impact points refer is the 17th board—the strike pocket.
- If your right-handed student rolled a hook ball perfectly along a 10-to-10 target line, but the ball hit the 4 pin slightly to the left of center, how would you instruct your student to move, using the 3-0-1-2 system, so that the next ball would (theoretically) hit directly in the strike pocket? The solution is simple if you use the fact that each observable pin (10, 6, 3, 1, 2, 4, 7) sits on every fifth lane board. Count the board numbers (1 through 39 from the right side if right handed or from the left side if you are left handed).
- First, determine near which numbered board the ball contacted the pins. The 4 pin is centered on board 30 (if you are right handed), but the off-center hit may have been on board 32.
- Since the desired point of impact is the pocket, or board number 17, the amount of error is 32 − 17 = 15 boards to the left of the strike pocket.
- Applying the 3-0-1-2 rule, we should divide 15 by 3 to yield 5. Then, we should multiply 5 by 2 to yield 10—the number of boards which the setup must be moved to the left.
- To test the adjustment, instruct your student to stand 10 boards further to the inside (the left for a right-handed bowler) and to use the same visual target as before.
- If the student executes properly and the ball rolls over the same target point at the level of the arrows, the ball should theoretically impact at the pocket.
- If the ball does not yield a pocket hit, determine the amount of error and correct the setup position again, using the 3-0-1-2 system.

Left-Handed Example

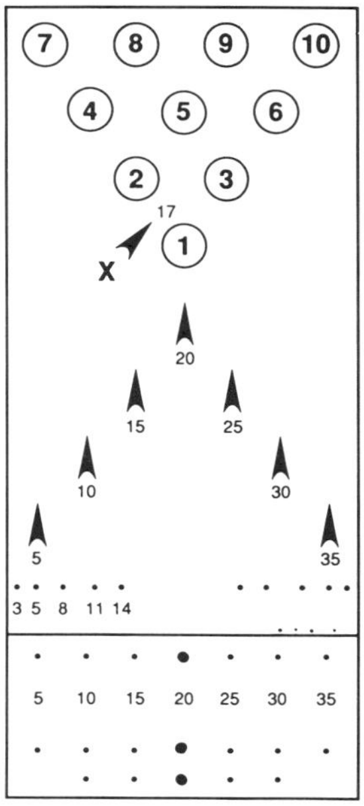

Right-Handed Example

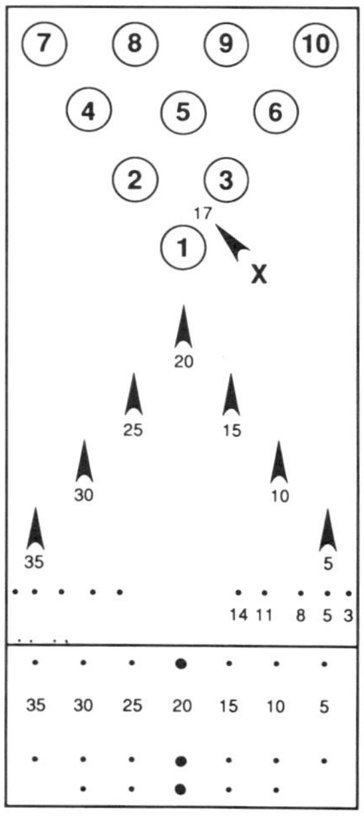

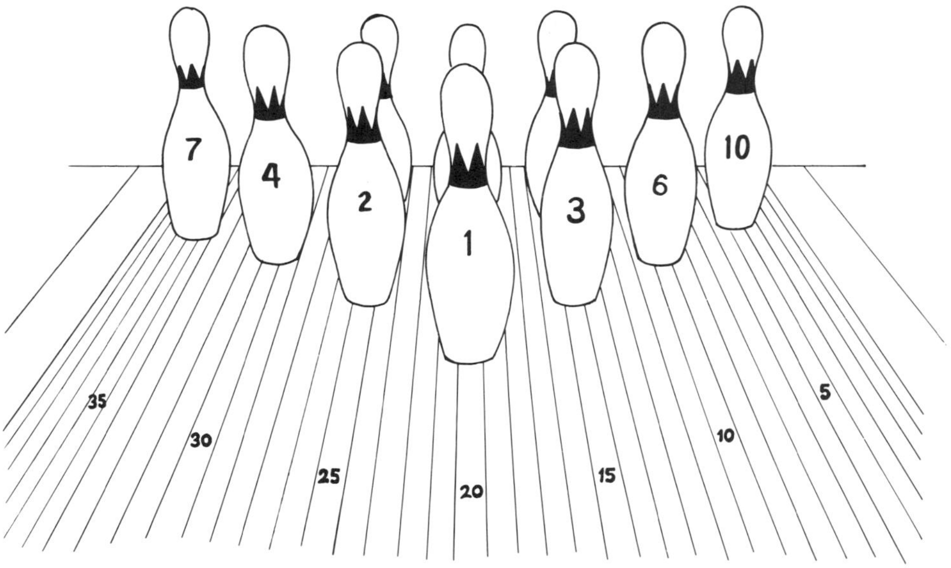

Right-Handed Example

Self-Testing

- Before you attempt to instruct a student in the 3-0-1-2 system, test yourself. Assume the following impact points of first balls for a right-handed bowler, and predict the proper number of boards and direction of setup location adjustments for a pocket impact on the next shot. Acceptable approximate answers are provided.
- *Impact*: Between the 2 and 4 pins.
  Adjustment: Board #27
  27 − 17 = 10;
  10 ÷ 3 = 3.3;
  3.3 × 2 = 6.6;
  7 boards to the inside of the original strike setup position
- *Impact*: Directly on the headpin.
  Adjustment: Board #20
  20 − 17 = 3;
  3 ÷ 3 = 1;
  1 × 2 = 2;
  2 boards to the inside of the original strike setup position
- *Impact*: Between the 3 and 6 pins.
  Adjustment: Board #12
  17 − 12 = 5;
  5 ÷ 3 = 1.6;
  1.6 × 2 = 3.2;
  3 boards to the outside of the original strike setup position
- *Impact*: Directly on the 3 pin.
  Adjustment: Board #14
  17 − 14 = 3;
  3 ÷ 3 = 1;
  1 × 2 = 2;
  2 boards to the outside of the original strike setup position
- *Impact*: Between the 1 and 2 pins.
  Adjustment: Board #22
  22 − 17 = 5;
  5 ÷ 3 = 1.6;
  1.6 × 2 = 3.2;
  3 boards to the inside of the original strike setup position

Adjusting for Any Spare

- The "base number" to which all impact points refer is the board number which the ball should pass over at impact with the spare.
- If your right-handed student was rolling the ball perfectly along a 10-to-10 target line, but left the 7 pin, how would you instruct your student to move, using the 3-0-1-2 system, to pick up the spare?
- First, determine which numbered board the 7 pin is on. This is board number 35—now the desired point of impact (left of the strike pocket).

- Assume that the visual target will still be the second arrow. Then, to determine how much your student must move the stance position, you first must know how far the 7 pin is from the pocket. The 7 pin is 35 − 17, or 18 boards to the left of the pocket.
- Applying the 3-0-1-2 rule, we should divide 18 by 3 to yield 6. Then, we should multiply 6 by 2 to yield 12—the number of boards which the normal setup must be moved to the right. Remember that the student's target line must cross the visual target and the desired 7 pin to make the spare.
- To test the adjustment, instruct your student to stand 12 boards further to the outside (the right for a right-handed bowler) and to use the same visual target as before.
- If the student executes properly and the ball rolls over the same target point at the level of the arrows, the ball should theoretically hit the 7 pin dead center.

Changing From One Arrow to Another

- When changing arrows, simply add or subtract 5 boards to *both* the target point and the setup location. For example, if you are shooting the 3 pin using the second arrow, but want to use the third arrow, simply shift the setup location 5 boards further to the inside, and use the third arrow as the target point.
- If you are using the third arrow, but want to use the second arrow to shoot the 7 pin, simply shift the setup location 5 boards further to the outside, and use the second arrow as the target point.

Step 7 Refine Pendulum Swing and Takeaway

The *takeaway* is the movement of the balance arm from supporting the ball in the fully extended pushaway to a position out from the body, slightly down and toward the back. The balance arm is held in this position throughout the delivery until the bowling arm completes the follow-through. You should help your students link the takeaway with the pendulum swing because the balance arm counterbalances some of the weight of the ball on the swingside, stabilizing the *pivot* for the swing and helping the back remain upright and the shoulders squared.

The coordinated pendulum swing and takeaway is no more difficult to refine than the pendulum swing by itself—if your students think of it as one coordinated movement. However, students in the same class will display many versions of the coordinated movement.

STUDENT KEYS TO SUCCESS

- Body stable before movement
- Ball falls into swing
- Balance arm moves with ball's fall
- Final balance arm position on count ''two''
- Body stable throughout

Coordinated Pendulum Swing and Takeaway Rating

CRITERION	BEGINNING LEVEL	ACCOMPLISHED LEVEL
Preparation	• Elbow bent, shoulders not square to foul line • Balance hand out of position	• Elbow straight, shoulders square to foul line • Balance hand in proper position
Execution	• Moves upper body to move ball in down-back-up cycle • Upper body pulled forward and down by weight of ball • Balance arm not in time	• Allows ball to freely fall into arc • Holds both shoulders stable • Balance arm starts on count ''one,'' out for count ''two''

Error Detection and Correction for Coordinated Pendulum Swing and Takeaway

Unless the balance arm in the takeaway is carefully timed with the fall of the ball into the swing, is consistently taken to the proper position, and is held in that position, delivery execution problems will occur. Take a position to the balance side for observing the following common errors.

ERROR	CORRECTION
1. Bowler takes the balance hand away too early.	1. Have your student wait until the count of "one" to begin the takeaway.
2. Bowler takes the balance hand away too late.	2. Tell your student to begin the takeaway as the ball starts to fall into the swing.
3. The bowler's balance arm moves to the wrong position during the takeaway.	3. Use the cue words "point to the wall." Show your student the proper out, down, and back position.
4. The bowler's balance arm moves after the takeaway.	4. Tell your student to hold the pointed position until the follow-through is completed.
5. The balance-arm elbow is bent at some time.	5. Have your student keep the balance-arm elbow straight from start to finish.

Pendulum Swing and Takeaway Coordination Drills

1. *Assisted Takeaway Coordination*

[Corresponds to *Bowling*, Step 7, Drill 1]

Group Management and Safety Tips

- This drill is best done with a pair of students per lane.
- Make sure that the partner supports the weight of the ball while the bowler is in the extension setup position.
- This drill is performed in a stationary position, using just the pendulum swing.

Instructions to Class

- "The goal of this drill is to coordinate the timing of the pendulum swing with the takeaway."
- "Assume your extension setup position, with your partner supporting the weight of the ball. Place your balance hand underneath your bowling hand. Stand erect in preparation for the ball to fall into the swing."
- "Count your swing cadence to yourself. When you're ready, say 'one.' "
- "Partners, when you hear 'one,' continue to count and let the ball fall into the swing."
- "As your ball begins its fall, remember to point your balance arm out, down, and back. Close your eyes and feel the relationship of timing between the movement of the ball falling into the swing and your balance arm moving into its proper position. Always match the speed of the takeaway to the ball's falling speed."
- "When your partner says 'two,' your balance arm should be in its final position, and should remain there throughout the remainder of the cadence."

Student Options

- "Alternately close and open your eyes to better sense the timing of the ball's position with your takeaway arm actions."
- "If you need to rest, switch roles with your partner after 5 attempts. Gradually work up to 10 consecutive swings."

Student Success Goal

- 10 consecutive coordinated swings and takeaways

To Decrease Difficulty

- Reduce the Success Goal to 6 or 8.
- Have student close eyes to meet the Success Goal.

To Increase Difficulty

- Have student use full delivery (eyes open) while partner observes timing.

2. *High and Low Takeaway Awareness*

[Corresponds to *Bowling*, Step 7, Drill 2]

Group Management and Safety Tips

- This drill is best done with a pair of students per lane.
- This drill is performed in a stationary position, using the pendulum swing from an extension setup position with a partner. It can be used to help students problem-solve their own errors.

Instructions to Class

- "This drill uses two improper takeaway positions to help you recognize and correct such errors quickly."
- "Repeat the previous drills, only this time move your balance arm about a foot higher than shoulder height. Concentrate on how the high takeaway affects your swingside shoulder."
- "Alternate five high takeaways with five correct takeaways."
- "Repeat this entire sequence with a low takeaway position by moving your balance hand directly to your balance side, your hand almost touching the side of your upper leg. Concentrate on the effects of this error on the position of your swingside shoulder. Then, alternate five low takeaways with five correct takeaways."

Student Options

- "Close your eyes to better sense the ball's position."
- "You and your partner may agree to mix the order of the three takeaway positions—high, low, and correct. You determine which to use in a given trial but do not inform your partner; ask your partner to identify which takeaway position was used."
- "You may complete the drill without a partner."

Student Success Goal

- 10 total takeaway height comparisons

  5 high with 5 correct takeaways and swings

  5 low with 5 correct takeaways and swings

To Decrease Difficulty

- Have student use only correct position.
- Have student close eyes to meet the Success Goal.

To Increase Difficulty

- Have student randomly mix the order of the three takeaways.
- Have student use full delivery while partner observes timing.

3. *Front and Back Takeaway Awareness*

[Corresponds to *Bowling,* Step 7, Drill 3]

Group Management and Safety Tips

- This drill is best done with a pair of students per lane.
- It is performed in a stationary position, using the pendulum swing from an extension setup position with a partner. It can be used to help students problem-solve their own errors.

Instructions to Class

- "As with the previous drill, the objective here is to deliberately deviate from the correct takeaway position so you can sense how the errors feel."
- "When the ball begins to go into the downswing at the count of 'one,' move your balance arm straight in front of its shoulder, as if you were reaching for something. Concentrate on the effects of this error on the position of your swingside shoulder. Alternate with correct takeaways for comparison."
- "Next, repeat the sequence, but use a back takeaway this time. When the ball begins to go into the downswing at the count of 'one,' move your balance arm directly behind the hip of your sliding leg. Concentrate on the effects of this error on the position of your swingside shoulder during the swing. Alternate with correct takeaways for comparison."

Student Options

- "Close your eyes to better sense the ball's position."
- "You and your partner may agree to mix these three takeaway positions—front, back, and correct. You determine which to use in a given trial but do not tell your partner. Ask your partner to identify the demonstrated position."
- "You may complete the drill without a partner."

Student Success Goal

- 10 total takeaway comparisons

  5 front with 5 correct takeaways and swings

  5 back with 5 correct takeaways and swings

To Decrease Difficulty

- Have student use only the correct position.
- Have student close eyes to meet the Success Goal.

To Increase Difficulty

- Have student randomly mix the order of the three takeaways.
- Have student use full delivery while partner observes timing.

4. 300 Drill

[Corresponds to *Bowling*, Step 7, Drill 4]

Group Management and Safety Tips

- This drill works well with a partner's evaluation.
- Remind students to focus on delivery execution instead of the actual number of pins knocked down.
- Refresh students on etiquette rules.

Instructions to Class

- "The purposes of this drill are to incorporate the timing of your pendulum swing and takeaway into your full delivery and to practice scoring a game. Continue to use your strike-targeting techniques, and don't worry about how many pins are actually knocked down."
- "With a partner, bowl a game according to the following rules: On your first delivery, if your partner says you demonstrated correct timing of your pendulum swing and takeaway arm, then you get a strike. If not, you get 9 points. On your second delivery, if you execute correctly, you get a spare. If not, mark a miss."
- "Alternate bowling one frame (two balls) with your partner, for a total of 10 frames. Tally your points (not pins) to get as close as possible to a perfect '300' game."

Student Option

- "You may also keep your pinfall score, but only your technique points count for the Success Goal."

Student Success Goal

- Bowl a game and get 225 out of 300 possible points

To Decrease Difficulty

- Reduce the Success Goal.

To Increase Difficulty

- Increase the Success Goal to 250 points.
- Have student bowl two games to demonstrate consistency in meeting the Success Goal.

Step 8 Refine Your Pushaway

The *pushaway* places the ball in the desired plane of the swing at a predetermined height, in line with the swing shoulder and a desired target. A properly executed pushaway encourages a free-pendulum swing, whereas an improperly executed pushaway hampers a free-pendulum swing.

Stress to your students the extreme importance of pushing the ball out sufficiently high, and in line with the shoulder and target, to take advantage of the potential energy of gravity, which provides natural ball speed. Pushaway errors are easily detected.

STUDENT KEYS TO SUCCESS

- Assume stable setup
- Push ball with both hands
- Balance arm carries most weight

Pushaway Rating

CRITERION	BEGINNING LEVEL	ACCOMPLISHED LEVEL
Preparation	• Shoulders not square to foul line • Ball not directly in line with shoulder, shakey	• Shoulders square to foul line • Ball in line with shoulder • Balance hand in proper position • Back straight
Execution	• Upper body pulled forward and down by ball • Pushaway slow and labored	• Back stable • Decisive push of ball • Arms extended on count "one"

Error Detection and Correction for the Pushaway

A properly executed pushaway promotes good timing and accuracy. Small errors in the direction of the pushaway can result in large errors at the point of impact with the pins in an actual delivery. The most common of all pushaway errors is *rounding off,* not pushing the ball horizontally to the elbows-extended position. The next most common error is allowing the shoulders to follow the ball forward and the head to move down as the ball is falling into the downswing.

ERROR	CORRECTION
Take a position to the student's swing-side to check for Errors 1 through 3.	
1. The student rounds off the pushaway, not fully extending horizontally.	1. Have your student support the ball with the balance hand during the pushaway and straighten the elbows before the ball begins moving down. Recommend Drill 1, Pushaway Placement and Coordination.
2. Bowler pushes away the ball too high.	2. Tell your student to push the ball no higher than shoulder level. Recommend Drill 2.
3. Bowler pushes away the ball too low.	3. Tell the student to push the ball to a level 2 to 3 inches higher than its level in the setup. Recommend Drill 2.
Move to a position directly in front of the student to check for Error 4.	
4. Bowler pushes away the ball too far to the inside or outside of the swing.	4. Have your student push the ball in line with the shoulder and the target on the lane. Recommend Drill 3.

Pushaway Drills

1. *Pushaway Placement and Coordination*

[Corresponds to *Bowling,* Step 8, Drill 1]

Group Management and Safety Tips

- This drill is best done with a pair of students per lane.
- Emphasize the necessity of gently pushing the ball into the partner's hands and of maintaining a standing, stationary position.

Instructions to Class

- "Assume a normal setup position facing your partner. Count your cadence through twice, then begin counting aloud."
- "Partners, hold your hands 2 to 3 inches higher than the ball is when the bowler is in setup position. Be ready to receive the ball when the bowler pushes it out."
- "Bowlers, on the count of 'four' be ready to push the ball so it arrives in your partner's waiting hands on count 'one'."
- "Check that your balance hand carries the ball's weight throughout the pushaway."

Student Options

- "Close your eyes to better sense the ball's position."
- "If you want to get a sense of how the upright back and shoulder girdle muscles support the pushaway, do the following with a partner. Hold both arms in front, elbows straight, palms up and one hand on top of the other. Partner holds arms the same, but with palms down and pushing on your palms. Mutually agree on the amount of resistance needed to feel the back muscles' support. This use of isometrics helps build strength, if necessary."

Student Success Goal

- 20 correctly placed and timed pushaways

To Decrease Difficulty

- Reduce the Success Goal.

To Increase Difficulty

- Achieve Success Goal without a partner.
- Add pendulum swing motion and cadence.
- Have student use full delivery while partner observes timing.

2. *High and Low Pushaway Awareness*

[Corresponds to *Bowling,* Step 8, Drill 2]

Group Management and Safety Tips

- This drill is best done with a pair of students per lane.
- Have partners adjust distance apart so that the bowler can push the ball gently into the partner's waiting hands.

Instructions to Class

- "Set up as in Drill 1."
- "Maintain a stationary position to focus on the effects that an excessively high or excessively low pushaway has on your posture and balance."

- "Alternately compare a high (1 to 2 feet higher) with a correct (straight from shoulder) pushaway."
- "Then, alternately compare a low (1 to 2 feet lower) with a correct (straight from shoulder) pushaway."

Student Options

- "Close your eyes to better sense the ball's position in relation to your upright posture and overall balance."
- "You and your partner may decide to mix the three pushaway destinations—high, low, and correct."

Student Success Goal

- 10 total pushaway height comparisons
  5 high with 5 correct pushaways
  5 low with 5 correct pushaways

To Decrease Difficulty

- Reduce Success Goal.

To Increase Difficulty

- Achieve Success Goal without a partner.
- Add pendulum swing motion.

3. *Inside and Outside Pushaway Awareness*

[Corresponds to *Bowling*, Step 8, Drill 3]

Group Management and Safety Tips

- This drill is best done with a pair of students per lane.
- Again, have bowlers adjust distance apart to avoid hitting waiting partners.

Instructions to Class

- "Set up as in the previous drill."
- "Maintain a stationary position in order to focus on the effects that an inside or outside pushaway has on your upright posture and overall balance."
- "Alternately compare an inside (6 to 8 inches farther inside) with a correct pushaway (straight from shoulder) direction."
- "Then, alternately compare an outside (6 to 8 inches farther outside) with a correct pushaway (straight from shoulder) direction."

Student Options

- "Close your eyes to better sense the ball's position in relationship to your upright posture and overall balance."
- "You and your partner may decide to mix the three pushaway directions—inside, outside, and correct."

Student Success Goal

- 10 total pushaway direction comparisons
  5 inside with 5 correct pushaways
  5 outside with 5 correct pushaways

To Decrease Difficulty

- Reduce the Success Goal.

To Increase Difficulty

- Achieve Success Goal without a partner.
- Add pendulum swing motion.

4. *Arm Splay Adjustment*

[New drill]

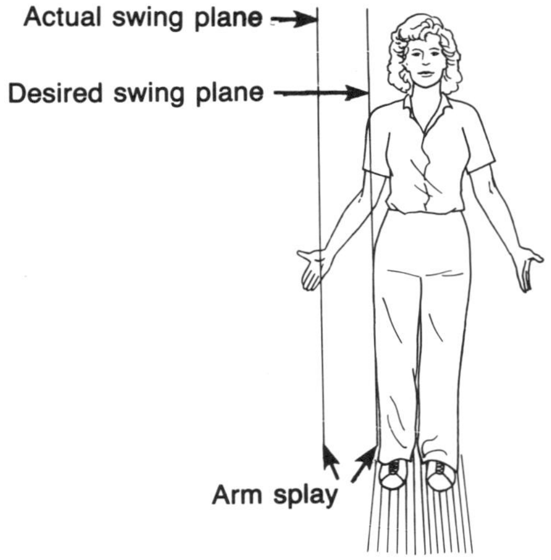

Group Management and Safety Tips

- This drill is optional, to be performed at your discretion. It is, however, desirable that you check each student and adjust the lateral ball position in the setup at some time.
- The objective of this drill is to check for arm splay and the possible need for adjustment of the lateral position of the ball in the setup. Otherwise, arm splay may induce the student to push the ball too far to the outside. This drill changes the pushaway destination of the ball by modifying its position in the setup.
- The splay, or deviation of the forearm, is best seen when the body is held in the accepted "anatomical" position.

Instructions to Individual

- "Hold your bowling arm at your side, straighten your elbow, and point your open palm to the front, your thumb pointed away from your body. (Note that your hand may be some distance away from your body. This characteristic, *arm splay*, is more common among females than males."
- "The greater the angle of arm splay, the farther the ball is away from the body during the downswing and forward swing. If the plane of the swing is too far from the body's center of gravity, the walking gait will be disturbed and maintaining good balance during the approach and follow-through may be difficult."
- "If a person with a sizable arm splay holds the ball directly in line with the shoulder during the setup and raises the upper arm in line with the shoulder during the pushaway, the forearm, hand, and ball will move toward the outside. Thus, the ball will begin to fall into a swing plane too far to the outside."
- "To avoid movement of the ball to the outside during the pushaway, align the ball slightly to the inside during the setup. Thus a 90-degree angle will be formed by the shoulders and a line between the bowling shoulder joint and the ball when the pushaway is completed."

Student Option

- Not applicable.

Student Success Goal

- Demonstrate correct pushaway (adjusted, if necessary)

To Decrease Difficulty

- Not applicable.

To Increase Difficulty

- Not applicable.

5. *300 Drill*

[Corresponds to *Bowling*, Step 8, Drill 4]

Group Management and Safety Tips

- This drill works well with a partner's evaluation.
- Remind students to focus on delivery execution instead of the actual number of pins knocked down.
- As necessary, refresh students on etiquette rules.

Instructions to Class

- ''The purposes of this drill are to incorporate the pushaway into your full delivery and to practice scoring a game. Continue to use your strike-targeting techniques, and don't worry about how many pins are actually knocked down.''
- ''With a partner, bowl a game according to the following rules: On your first delivery, if your partner says you correctly demonstrated the pushaway, then you get a strike. If not, you get 8 points. On your second delivery, if you execute correctly, you get a spare. If not, mark a miss.''
- ''Alternate bowling one frame (two balls) with your partner for a total of 10 frames. Tally your points (not pins) to get as close as possible to a '300' game.''

Student Option

- ''You may also keep your pinfall score, but only your technique points count for the Success Goal.''

Student Success Goal

- Bowl a game and get 225 out of 300 possible points

To Decrease Difficulty

- Reduce the Success Goal.

To Increase Difficulty

- Increase the Success Goal to 250 points.
- Have students bowl two games to demonstrate consistency in meeting the Success Goal.

Step 9 Refine Three Skills

If your students have successfully executed the pushaway then they will have little difficulty refining the pushaway, the pendulum swing, and the takeaway into fluid, rhythmical movements that match their cadence. At first it is helpful to isolate and practice coordinating these upper-body movements without adding lower-body movements. Whether feet are stationary or moving, your students will still display execution differences.

STUDENT KEYS TO SUCCESS

- Body stable before movement
- Push ball out with both hands
- Ball falls into swing
- Balance arm moves with swing
- Body stable and squared

Pushaway/Pendulum Swing/Takeaway Coordination Drills

1. Upper Body Coordination

[Corresponds to *Bowling*, Step 9, Drill 1]

Group Management and Safety Tips

- This is a solo drill.
- Remind students to check for clearance so as not to injure themselves or anyone around them.
- While remaining stationary, students should continue to use the second arrow from the outside of the lane as their visual fixation point, using it and their bowling shoulders as reference points for their swing planes.

Instructions to Class

- ''Assume a normal setup position. Count your swing cadence to yourself.''
- ''Using only your upper body movements, check your timing by doing the following: Properly push the ball away so that on count 'one' your elbows are straight. As the ball begins to fall, do a correct takeaway. On count 'two' the ball reaches the bottom of the swing and the balance hand reaches its final destination. On count 'three' the ball reaches the top of the backswing. On count 'four' the ball passes your swingside on the way forward. On count 'four' begin to return your balance hand to meet the ball.''
- ''Finish in normal setup position.''
- ''Alternate doing the drill with your eyes open and closed. Concentrate on the timing of all movements.''

Student Option

- ''You may ask a partner to count with you to help check your timing accuracy.''

Student Success Goal

- 5 consecutive coordinated swings
  3 with eyes open
  2 with eyes closed

To Decrease Difficulty

- Allow a "dry-run" drill using no ball.
- If student stops or clips the ball at the top of the backswing, help him or her be aware of an exaggerated forward lean by tapping the ball as it rises into the backswing.
- Have students close eyes.

To Increase Difficulty

- Increase the Success Goal.

2. *Assisted Troubleshooting*

[Corresponds to *Bowling*, Step 9, Drill 2]

Group Management and Safety Tips

- This drill is best done with a pair of students per lane.
- Again, students remain stationary.

Instructions to Class

- "Repeat the sequence of movements you just did. This time your partner helps evaluate your form."
- "Partners, as you observe a characteristic, place a check in the appropriate column in your partner's book. Observe only one characteristic per trial."
- "If you have trouble with any particular aspect of the sequence, repeat the previous drill."

Student Option

- "Select between 5 and 10 repetitions to practice at your own pace before your partner begins evaluating you."

Student Success Goal

- Demonstrate all 5 movement characteristics from participant's book correctly

To Decrease Difficulty

- Repeat previous drill.

To Increase Difficulty

- Not applicable.

3. *300 Drill*

[Corresponds to *Bowling*, Step 9, Drill 3]

Group Management and Safety Tips

- This drill works well with a partner's evaluation.
- Remind students to focus on delivery execution instead of the actual number of pins knocked down.
- As necessary, refresh students on etiquette rules.

Instructions to Class

- "The purposes of this drill are to incorporate the pushaway, pendulum swing, and takeaway into your full delivery and to practice scoring a game. Continue to use your strike-targeting techniques, and don't worry about how many pins are actually knocked down."

- ''With a partner, bowl a game according to the following rules: On your first delivery, if your partner says you correctly coordinated the pushaway, pendulum swing, and takeaway, then you get a strike. If not, you get 7 points. On your second delivery, if you execute correctly, you get a spare. If not, mark a miss.''
- ''Alternate bowling one frame (two balls) with your partner for a total of 10 frames. Tally your points (not pins) to get as close as possible to a '300' game.''

Student Option

- ''You may also keep your pinfall score, but only your technique points count for the Success Goal.''

Student Success Goal

- Bowl a game and get 225 out of 300 possible points

To Decrease Difficulty

- Reduce the Success Goal.

To Increase Difficulty

- Increase the Success Goal to 250 points.
- Have students bowl two games to demonstrate consistency in meeting the Success Goal.

Step 10 Refine First Step and Pushaway

Coordination between the first step and the pushaway is one of the most difficult movements for students to learn and to continue to perform correctly, no matter what their level of skill or experience.

To fail to fully extend the pushaway horizontally, to round off, results in various degrees of swing tension. Rounding off causes the ball to be early with respect to the steps, so muscular tension is used, consciously or unconsciously, to slow the swing down so the steps can ''catch up'' with the ball.

Stress to your students that in an actual delivery, it is extremely important to extend the pushaway, straightening both arms, before the bowling arm moves down into the swing. Also stress that during the first step there is only the pushaway, a horizontal motion. There should be no downward motion of the ball during the first step. The swing takes place during the second, third, and fourth counts.

STUDENT KEYS TO SUCCESS

- Assume stable setup
- Begin on the ''AND'' after ''four''
- First step and extended arms on ''one''

Error Detection and Correction for Coordinated First Step and Pushaway

A very frequent error that affects the delivery is *late ball,* the ball arriving at the release point later than the sliding foot. Another common error is *early ball,* the ball arriving at the release before the sliding foot. This latter error causes a hop between the second and third steps (in the four-step delivery) as well as a loss of lift with the fingers at the release. Early pushaway can cause either early or late ball; late pushaway almost invariably causes late ball. When you are observing the timing between the pushaway and the first step—especially at close range—train your eyes on your student's feet and catch sight of the pushaway in your peripheral vision. Do not expect to focus on the pushaway and also see the feet; you will not see what you are looking for.

Take a position to the swingside of the student to check for all the following errors.

ERROR

1. First step is taken on the toe or with a shuffle.

2. Ball is pushed away too slow or after the first step has begun.

3. Ball is pushed away too fast or earlier than the foot begins to move.

CORRECTION

1. Tell the student to step out by lifting the foot off of the approach as if taking a walk. Give the cue ''heel-toe.''

2. Have your student push the ball faster—not sooner—than the first step. Be sure that the ball and foot start moving at exactly the same instant! See Drills 2 and 3.

3. Remind your student to begin the push with the step and to regulate the speed of the pushaway so that the ball reaches the locked-elbows position as the heel touches down on ''one.'' See Drills 2 and 4.

ERROR	CORRECTION
4. Ball is pushed too far to the inside.	4. Have bowler review Step 8.

5. Ball is pushed too far to the outside.	5. Have bowler review Step 8.

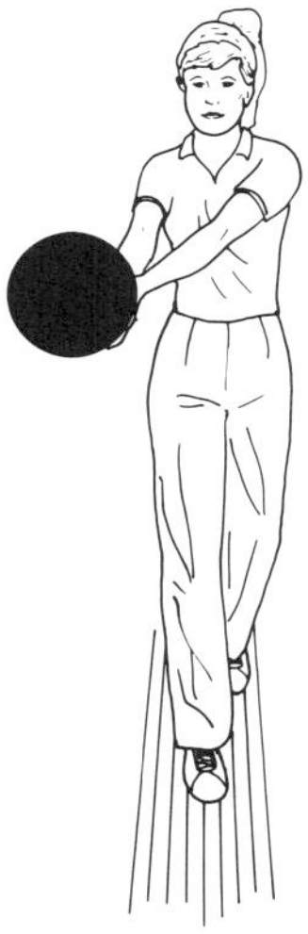

ERROR	**CORRECTION**
6. Ball is pushed too high.	6. Have bowler review Step 8.

7. Ball is pushed too low.	7. Have bowler review Step 8.

First Step and Pushaway Coordination Drills

1. *No-Ball Coordination*

[Corresponds to *Bowling,* Step 10, Drill 1]

Group Management and Safety Tips

- A pair of students work per lane.
- Remind students to allow partners additional room when the first step is taken.
- Do not use bowling balls in this drill.
- Use this drill only as a review. Many students may be able to start with the next drill.

Instructions to Class

- "Without a ball, run through your usual series of setup checks."
- "Your partner should hold one palm up, like a traffic officer signaling a stop, 2 to 3 inches higher than your hands in your setup position to represent your pushaway destination."
- "To sharpen your concept of timing, be sure to use an 'AND' halfway between cadence counts."
- "On the 'AND' after 'four,' begin your push and your step. Push your bowling arm out crisply with your balance hand. Step out slowly with your swingside foot. Do not move your balance-side, or sliding, foot."
- "On 'one,' the backs of your bowling fingers touch your partner's palm and your heel touches down on the approach. Both elbows are at the extended position."
- "Concentrate on the imaginary click of 'locking' your elbows, the real tap of your swingside heel, and the pat of your fingers on your partner's palm—all occurring at the same instant (perfect timing)."

Student Option

- "Decide rotation order with your partner."

Student Success Goal

- 25 consecutive well-timed repetitions

To Decrease Difficulty

- Lower the Success Goal.

To Increase Difficulty

- Not applicable.

2. *Ball Coordination*

[Corresponds to *Bowling,* Step 10, Drill 2]

Group Management and Safety Tips

- A pair of students work per lane.
- Allow sufficient space between partners for one step and for placing the ball into the partner's hands.

Instructions to Class

- "This drill helps you develop the back muscles involved in transporting your ball to the fully extended pushaway position as well as refine your timing."

- "Use a ball and assume a normal setup position with your partner facing you."
- "Begin counting your cadence, stressing each 'AND.' Begin your push and first step on the 'AND' after 'four.' Push your bowling arm out crisply with your balance hand. Step out slowly with your swing-side foot. Do not move your balance-side foot."
- "On 'one,' the ball arrives in your partner's hands, your heel touches down, and both elbows are in an extended position. Concentrate on the imaginary click of your elbows, the real tap of your swingside heel, and the arrival of your ball in your partner's hands—all occurring at the same instant."

Student Option

- "Decide rotation order with your partner."

Student Success Goal

- 25 consecutive well-timed step and push-away combinations

To Decrease Difficulty

- Lower the Success Goal.

To Increase Difficulty

- Not applicable.

3. *Late Ball Timing Awareness*

[Corresponds to *Bowling*, Step 10, Drill 3]

Group Management and Safety Tip

- A pair of students work per lane.

Instructions to Class

- "Assume a normal setup position with your partner facing you."
- "Repeat the sequence of movements of the last drill for the correct timing."
- "To create a late pushaway step out on the 'AND' after 'four,' but wait until the count of 'one' to begin your pushaway. On 'one,' your heel touches down on the approach, but your ball arrives (elbows extended) in your partner's hands later."
- "Concentrate on the awkward feel of a late pushaway. You may find yourself pushing the ball away faster to catch up with your step."

Student Option

- After each late pushaway, select between 5 and 10 correctly timed pushaways to practice at your own pace."

Student Success Goal

- 5 late pushaways alternating with 5 correctly timed pushaways for comparison

To Decrease Difficulty

- Use only correctly timed pushaways.
- Lower the Success Goal.

To Increase Difficulty

- Have student use a full delivery while partner observes timing. Small errors magnify when footwork is added.

4. *Early Ball Timing Awareness*

[Corresponds to *Bowling*, Step 10, Drill 4]

Group Management and Safety Tip

- A pair of students work per lane.

Instructions to Class

- "Assume a normal setup position with your partner facing you."
- "Repeat the sequence of movement of Drill 2 for the correct timing."
- "To create an early pushaway, begin your pushaway on the 'AND' after 'four,' but wait until the count of 'one' to step out with your swingside foot. On 'one,' your ball arrives in your partner's hands, but your heel touches down on the approach later."
- "Concentrate on the awkward feel of an early pushaway. You may find yourself being pulled by the ball toward your partner. This feeling is a reflection of your center of gravity moving to a point in front of your body; your body feels that it must move forward faster to regain balance."

Student Option

- "After each early pushaway, select between 5 and 10 correctly timed pushaways to practice at your own pace."

Student Success Goal

- 5 early pushaways alternating with 5 correctly timed pushaways for comparison

To Decrease Difficulty

- Use only correctly timed pushaways.
- Lower the Success Goal.

To Increase Difficulty

- Have student use a full delivery while partner observes timing. Small errors magnify when footwork is added.

5. *300 Drill*

[Corresponds to *Bowling*, Step 10, Drill 5]

Group Management and Safety Tips

- This drill works well with a partner's evaluation.
- Remind students to focus on delivery execution instead of the actual number of pins knocked down.
- As necessary, refresh students on etiquette rules.

Instructions to Class

- "The purposes of this drill are to incorporate your perfectly timed first step with your pushaway into your full delivery and to practice scoring a game. Continue to use your strike-targeting techniques, and don't worry about how many pins are actually knocked down."

- "With a partner, bowl a game according to the following rules: On your first delivery, if your partner says you correctly coordinated your first step with your pushaway, then you get a strike. If not, you get 6 points. On your second delivery, if you execute correctly, you get a spare. If not, mark a miss."
- "Alternate bowling one frame (two balls) with your partner for a total of 10 frames. Tally your points (not pins) to get as close as possible to a '300' game."

Student Option

- "You may also keep your pinfall score, but only your technique points count for your Success Goal."

Student Success Goal

- Bowl a game and get 225 out of 300 possible points

To Decrease Difficulty

- Reduce the Success Goal.

To Increase Difficulty

- Increase the Success Goal to 250 points.
- Have students bowl two games to demonstrate consistency in meeting the Success Goal.

Step 11 Refine Four Skills

The coordinated trial delivery combines both upper- and lower-body movements. In particular, the gait establishes the stable base of support needed for your students to apply finger leverage (power) to the ball. The finish is not detailed here because it is important and extensive enough to practice on its own. You can use this step to ''clean up'' any timing difficulties your students are having with their deliveries before introducing the details of the finish.

STUDENT KEYS TO SUCCESS

- Upright and squared before movement
- Pushaway timed with first step
- Slow steps in time with swing
- Unhurried last step
- Slide in time with ball

Error Detection and Correction for the Coordinated Trial Delivery

Actual delivery errors are usually caused by improper timing between the ball and the footwork and in the speed with which the steps are taken. The most common error, fast feet, although mostly an error in footwork, becomes more blatant when the swinging ball is added.

You will find that the following errors occur quite frequently when your students attempt full deliveries. Take a position to the back and swingside of the student to check for all the following errors.

ERROR	**CORRECTION**
1. The steps are taken too fast (fast feet); the ball arrives at the foul line after the sliding foot.	1. Slow the feet, matching the footwork to the cadence. Also check for a late pushaway timing problem. This often goes unnoticed by students.

2. There is a hop in the delivery, usually between the second and third steps. (This is actually not a hop, but a hesitation of the ball at the top of the backswing, with a corresponding hesitation between the second and third steps.) The ball may arrive at the foul line before the sliding foot.	2. Check for an early pushaway timing problem.
3. The bowler hesitates between each of the steps.	3. Have your student make the movement flow; do not allow him or her to stop—even momentarily—on each count.
4. Bowler walks in an irregular path to the foul line, and experiences target-hitting inaccuracies.	4. This is not a typical "style" deviation. Check for either an inside or an outside pushaway deviation.
5. Bowler muscles the ball, causing the ball to be late with respect to the steps. Bowler seems to persistently miss the desired target.	5. Check for too-high, too-low, early, or late pushaway errors.

Coordinated Trial Delivery Drills

1. *Unassisted Trial Delivery*

[Corresponds to *Bowling*, Step 11, Drill 1]

Group Management and Safety Tip

- This is a solo drill.

Instructions to Class

- "Assume a normal setup position and begin your cadence, including the 'AND' between each count."
- "Execute a coordinated trial delivery to refine your timing coordination between your upper- and lower-body movements. Refer to your text for a detailed summary and a list of evaluative characteristics."
- "Report two well-executed repetitions for each characteristic. Give yourself one point for each characteristic felt."

Student Option

- "You may ask a partner to evaluate your technique and compare results."

Student Success Goal

- 15 out of 20 possible points

To Decrease Difficulty

- Have student start from an extended pushaway position, while you stand to his or her swingside and hold the weight of the student's ball in both your hands. Be prepared to move forward with the student. Count cadence out loud. On your signal, student may begin walking forward. Stop the delivery if you notice any of the following as the first step is taken: excessive arm tension; attempts to either lift the ball up or push the ball down; or bending the swingside elbow. Just as the student is beginning the second step, let the ball fall into the swing. Provide appropriate feedback.

To Increase Difficulty

- Increase the Success Goal.

2. *Arm and Leg Length Compensation*

[New drill]

Group Management and Safety Tips

- This drill is optional and at your discretion. It is, however, desirable that you check each student, especially if you observe persistent timing difficulties. If so, it may be necessary to adjust the vertical position of the ball in the setup to compensate for an excessively long or short bowling arm.
- Make sure that the student is executing properly. Record your impression of the timing of the student's ball and steps at each of the following setup levels. As necessary, recommend that a permanent vertical ball position in the setup be adopted.

Use the following abbreviations as entries: IT = in time, L = ball is late, E = ball is early.

Pushaway level	Timing
Usual position	________
3 inches higher than usual	________
3 inches lower than usual	________
6 inches higher than usual	________
6 inches lower than usual	________

Instructions to Individual

- ''A short bowling arm means that the ball takes less time to move through the shorter arc of the swing. A longer arm means that the ball takes more time to complete the longer arc.''
- ''A bowler with relatively short arms and long legs must push the ball away higher, creating a longer swing arc, to accommodate the longer legs. A bowler with relatively long arms and short legs must push the ball away lower, creating a shorter arc, to accommodate the shorter legs.''
- ''To effectively adjust your vertical ball setup position to accommodate the length of your bowling arm, first, take 3 normal setups and deliveries with your ball held in the usual setup position. It is important that you push the ball straight out horizontally from the starting level.''
- ''Next, take 3 normal setups and deliveries with your ball held 3 inches *higher* than usual. Then take 3 normal setups and deliveries with your ball held 3 inches *lower* than usual.''
- ''Lastly, take 3 normal setups and deliveries with your ball held 6 inches *higher* than usual. Then take 3 normal setups and deliveries with your ball held 6 inches *lower* than usual.''
- ''Choose the height of the pushaway that corrects your timing problem and use that height for all future deliveries.''

Student Option

- Not applicable.

Student Success Goal

- Demonstrate an appropriate vertical ball position in the setup

To Decrease Difficulty

- Not applicable.

To Increase Difficulty

- Not applicable.

3. 300 Drill

[Corresponds to *Bowling*, Step 11, Drill 2]

Group Management and Safety Tips

- This drill works well with a partner's evaluation.
- Remind students to focus on delivery execution instead of the number of pins knocked down.
- As necessary, refresh students on etiquette rules.

Instructions to Class

- ''The purposes of this drill are to incorporate both upper- and lower-body movements into your full delivery and to practice scoring a game. Continue to use your strike-targeting techniques and don't worry about how many pins are actually knocked down.''

- ''With a partner, bowl a game according to the following rules: On your first delivery, if your partner says you correctly demonstrated a coordinated trial delivery, then you get a strike. If not, you get 5 points. On your second delivery, if you execute correctly, you get a spare. If not, mark a miss.''
- ''Alternate bowling one frame (two balls) with your partner for a total of 10 frames. Tally your points (not pins) to get as close as possible to a '300' game.''

Student Option

- ''You may also keep your pinfall score, but only your technique points count for the Success Goal.''

Student Success Goal

- Bowl a game and get 225 out of 300 possible points

To Decrease Difficulty

- Reduce the Success Goal.

To Increase Difficulty

- Increase the Success Goal to 250 points.
- Have students bowl two games to demonstrate consistency in meeting the Success Goal.

Step 12 Finish

The *finish* is the collective, coordinated motions of the upper and lower body from the swing-side foot's touching down in preparation for the slide, to the completed follow-through. The practice finish is a *one-step delivery* composed of the setup; the coordinated pushaway, pendulum swing, and takeaway; and the power push.

Stress to your students that the finish is the most important segment of the delivery. A good finish is the reward for proper execution of the setup and first three steps of the delivery; a bad finish is also the penalty for poor execution. The finish is significant to the performer because it provides the greatest opportunity for feedback on the quality of execution. For this reason, a large ''Error Detection and Correction'' section is included.

STUDENT KEYS TO SUCCESS

- Upright and squared before movement
- Full pushaway, pendulum swing, and takeaway
- Begin slide as ball reaches top
- Slide forward with ball
- Take unhurried release
- Finish in sitting-tall position

Finish Rating

CRITERION	BEGINNING LEVEL	ACCOMPLISHED LEVEL
Preparation	• Shoulders not square • Ball not held in proper position • Knees bent or elbows flared out	• Shoulders square • Ball in proper position • Elbows held in, back and knees straight
Execution	• Steps forward on heel • Leans body forward • Steps out too soon as ball is still going to top of backswing • Knee bend is early	• Slides out on sole • Back and shoulders erect and stable • Ball in time with foot • Knee bend begins after ball has reached top of backswing
Recovery	• Leans forward, off balance, or shaky • Knees not sufficiently bent • Arms in wrong positions • Follow-through weak and uncertain	• Back straight • Knees bent deeply • Arms in proper positions • Obviously strong, sitting posture

Error Detection and Correction for the Finish

Errors in the path of the rolled ball during an actual delivery result largely from errors in the finish. The most common finish errors are taking the last step and slide too fast, muscling the ball forward from the downswing, leaning the upper body too far forward, and failing to bend the knees sufficiently.

ERROR	CORRECTION
Take a position to the student's swing-side to check for Errors 1 through 6.	
1. The bowler is stepping, not sliding, forward to the foul line.	1. Remind your student not to lift the sliding foot off the approach as the ball starts down.
2. The bowler slides forward too fast.	2. Tell the student to match the speed of the slide to the ball's forward swing; remind him or her not to rush.
3. The bowler slides forward too soon.	3. Urge your student to wait until the ball is motionless at the top of the backswing before starting the forward slide.
4. The bowler leans over, bending too far at the waist.	4. Remind the student to keep the back upright by lowering the hips.
5. The bowler lofts the ball, tossing the ball too far out onto the lane.	5. Check the student's ball grip first. If the grip is acceptable, remind the student to keep the wrist firm, not to grip the ball too tightly, and to let the ball swing forward by its own weight. Also check for an early pushaway.

ERROR

6. The bowler muscles the forward swing, ''yanking the ball down.''

CORRECTION

6. Tell the student to roll the ball easily by allowing it to swing forward by its own momentum. You may need to assist the student's forward swing. In preparation, have your student count the cadence aloud once, then begin a one-step delivery. As the ball starts down into the forward swing of the one-step delivery, *gently* and carefully seize your student's wrist and direct the arm forward at the proper speed, ending in the fully extended follow-through position. Do not step too close; watch the ball throughout so that you will not be hit.

ERROR | **CORRECTION**

Move to a position directly behind the student to check for Errors 7 through 10.

Error: 7. The bowler drops the bowling shoulder.

Correction: 7. Tell the student to keep the shoulders level by stretching the balance arm out, down, and back. You may need to assist the timing and placement of the student's balance arm. Have your student prepare to execute a one-step delivery as you stand on the student's balance side. Do not stand too close; avoid being hit by the balance hand. Signal the student to count the cadence aloud once, then begin. As the ball starts down from the extended pushaway position, *gently* seize your student's balance arm at the wrist. Direct the arm at the proper speed into the proper position by count''two.'' Hold this balance-arm position throughout the follow-through position.

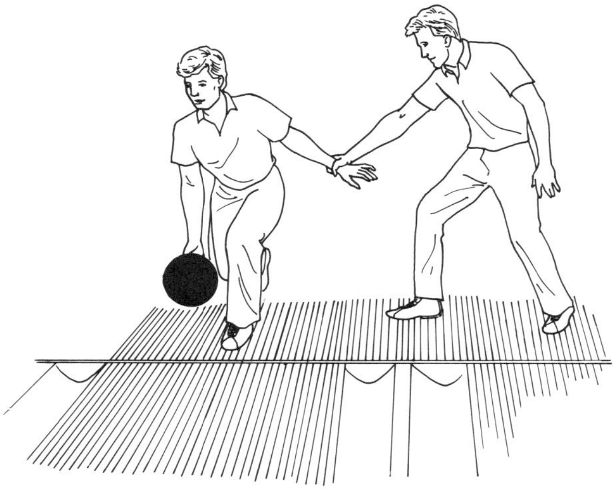

ERROR	**CORRECTION**
8. The bowler ''double-bounces'' ball: the ball hits the approach before the release.	8. Point out to your student that he or she may be leaning over. Demonstrate lowering the hips while keeping the back upright and the shoulders level. Remind the student not to lunge. As a novelty, you could ask the student to deliver the ball while kneeling on a folded towel. 
9. The bowler raises the hips (''rearing up'') during the downswing. 	9. Tell the student to keep the back upright and let the ball swing forward by its own momentum. Remind him or her not to muscle the ball. Check the ball fit for insecure thumb grip; the student is probably losing the ball off of the thumb midway through the slide.

ERROR	CORRECTION
10. The student steps over to the swingside after the release (a "fallaway").	10. Demonstrate the deep bend of the swingside leg during the slide.

Finish Drills

1. *Power Push Delivery*

[Corresponds to *Bowling,* Step 12, Drill 1]

Group Management and Safety Tips

- This drill is best done in pairs.
- As appropriate, remind your students to always check for clearance on both sides.
- To emphasize the feel of the finish, you may need to assist students as appropriate to their weakness, such as an early or late pushaway, an improperly placed takeaway arm, and so forth. A strong finish position promotes a feeling of stability, giving a strong feeling of leverage to the fingers.
- Occasionally a student may have difficulty maintaining traction with the swingside foot if the sole is not made of rubber or if it has a leather tip. If this is the case, refer the student to a professional shoe repairman, who can cover the entire sole with nonmarring rubber. Caution against using plastic or crepe.

Instructions to Class

- "Everything you do from your setup through your first three steps is simply preparation for a strong, well-balanced finish."
- "A good finish allows you consistently accurate projection of your ball onto the lane with more power because you are using the larger and stronger muscles of your back and legs to do the job, while holding your shoulders perpendicular to your swing plane."
- "Assume a setup position about 4 feet from the foul line, facing the second arrow."
- "Count your cadence and focus on your visual target. From a stationary position, execute a normal pushaway and let the ball fall into its pendulum swing. On the 'AND' after 'three,' begin lifting your sliding foot off the approach and bending your swingside knee. On the count of 'four,' use your swingside sole as an anchor and push your sliding foot forward. On the 'AND' after 'four,' allow your center of gravity to move down as your sliding foot continues forward. Release your ball on the upswing."
- "Practice a few times, then do two well-executed, one-step deliveries for each characteristic on the chart in your book."
- "Have your partner evaluate you, then compare your recall of a characteristic with your partner's assessment."
- "Again, your ideal finishing body orientation is sitting tall—a position of potential power. You must stabilize your body at the finish so that it can effectively support the forward swing and release. Your feet should be apart, your shoulders and hips perpendicular to your swing, and your back straight as you are releasing your ball."

Student Option

- "Decide rotation order with your partner."

Student Success Goal

- 15 out of 20 total points

To Decrease Difficulty

- Assist the student without a ball. Stand to your student's swingside, and have student count cadence aloud. On your signal, gently direct the student's bowling arm through the motions of the pushaway, the fall of the ball, the downswing, the backswing, and the forward swing of a one-step delivery. As necessary, slow down the student's cadence, then build to proper speed. Ask the student to start his or her slide just as the bowling arm reaches the top of the backswing, slide smoothly, keep the back foot on the approach, finish in the sitting-tall position, and hold the follow-through position (see Figure 12.1a, b).

To Increase Difficulty

- Not applicable.

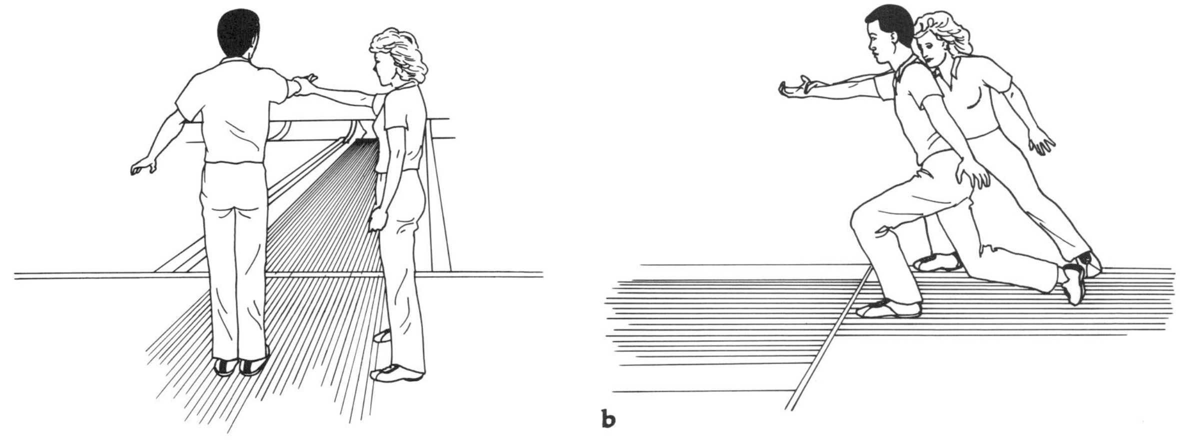

a b

Figure 12.1 Assisted one-step finish without the ball.

2. 300 Drill

[Corresponds to *Bowling*, Step 12, Drill 2]

Group Management and Safety Tips

- This drill works well with partners' evaluation.
- Remind students to focus on delivery execution versus how many actual pins are knocked down.
- As necessary, refresh students on etiquette rules.

Instructions to Class

- "The purposes of this drill are to incorporate a high-quality finish into your full delivery, and to practice scoring a game. Continue to use your strike-targeting techniques, and don't worry about how many actual pins are knocked down."
- "With a partner, bowl a game according to the following rules: On your first delivery, if your partner says you correctly demonstrated a high-quality finish, then you get a strike. If not, you get 4 points. On your second delivery, if you execute correctly, you get a spare. If not, mark a miss."
- "Alternate bowling one frame (two balls) with your partner for a total of 10 frames. Tally your points (not pins) to get as close as possible to a '300' game."

Student Option

- "You may count both pins and points."

Student Success Goal

- Bowl a game and get 225 out of 300 possible points.

To Decrease Difficulty

- Reduce the Success Goal.

To Increase Difficulty

- Increase the Success Goal to 250 points.
- Have students bowl 2 games to demonstrate consistency in meeting the Success Goal.

Step 13 Refine Five Skills

A coordinated finished delivery represents the most efficient delivery your students can execute. It incorporates five skills: the pendulum swing, the takeaway, the pushaway, proper footwork, and the finish. It should contain no wasted movements, and be consistently reproduced with ease. The main objectives now are to help each student

1. simplify the concept of the delivery,
2. make the delivery flow more freely,
3. combine a coordinated trial delivery with the finish, and
4. get an opportunity to exhibit his or her optimum technique.

At this point, your students should be able to troubleshoot common errors. If you want to show advanced students or help interested students with persistent coordination problems understand how to deliver a ball using a varied step-number approach, see Drill 4.

STUDENT KEYS TO SUCCESS

- Stable before movement
- Pushaway with first step
- Steps in time with swing
- Unhurried last step
- Slide in time with ball
- Powerful push to line
- Sitting-tall finish

Finished Delivery Drills

1. *Simplified Cue Delivery*

[Corresponds to *Bowling*, Step 13, Drill 1]

Group Management and Safety Tip

- This is a solo drill.

Instructions to Class

- "No instructor or coach expects a performer to remember all cues at all times; 'paralysis by analysis' is always a possibility!"
- "To help you make your movements more automatic and flowing, you should follow a shortened sequence of cues leading to finished delivery. Look back briefly at the Keys to Success shown in Figure 13.1 in your book. The list of cues presented there is shortened to help you combine movements and increase your overall smoothness."
- "For every setup, use the two cues listed under 'Preparation Phase' in your book. Lock in strongly on your visual target, using it as a stabilizer for your head, and count your cadence for consistency. For the 'Execution Phase,' take three deliveries for each of the six simplified cues [following], thinking only of coordinating the listed actions with the appropriate counts during your delivery. Make your movements flow. For the 'Recovery Phase,' use the two cues, 'sit tall' and 'follow-through square,' for every delivery."

Execution Phase

1. **Count "AND" after "four":**
   - Push ball out
   - Step out
2. **Count "one":**
   - Elbows straight
   - Heel down
   - Let it fall
   - Walk tall
3. **Count "two":**
   - Point to wall
   - Heel down
   - Ball low
   - Walk tall
4. **Count "three":**
   - Heel down
   - Ball high
   - Walk tall
5. **Count "AND" after "three":**
   - Let it fall
6. **Count "four":**
   - Push into slide
   - Sole down
   - Release ball
   - Continue slide

Student Option

- "Select between 12 and 24 deliveries to practice at your own pace."

Student Success Goal

- 18 deliveries, 3 deliveries per count under "Execution Phase" of Figure 13.1

To Decrease Difficulty

- Have student increase the number of deliveries per count.

To Increase Difficulty

- Have student bowl a game and rate delivery timing coordination on a scale of 1 (low) to 5 (high).

2. *How Good Is Your Form?*

[Corresponds to *Bowling,* Step 13, Drill 2]

Group Management and Safety Tips

- Two students work per lane, one performing and one observing from behind.
- You may use the characteristics listed in the participant's book and/or select characteristics representative of good form for your class members to observe.
- Scan your class, being especially observant for fallaway at the finish.
- Observation tip: You can detect late ball—the ball's arriving later than the sliding foot at the foul line—by the angle of the sliding foot at the foul line. The more the toe is pointed toward the swingside, the later the ball was in the delivery. For most bowlers, if the ball is in time with the steps, the hips remain perpendicular to the swing, and the sliding toe points slightly toward the balance side, away from the swing. If the ball is late relative to the steps, the swingside hip moves toward the back during the finish, countering the force of the ball's moving down and forward, thus pointing the toe toward the swing.

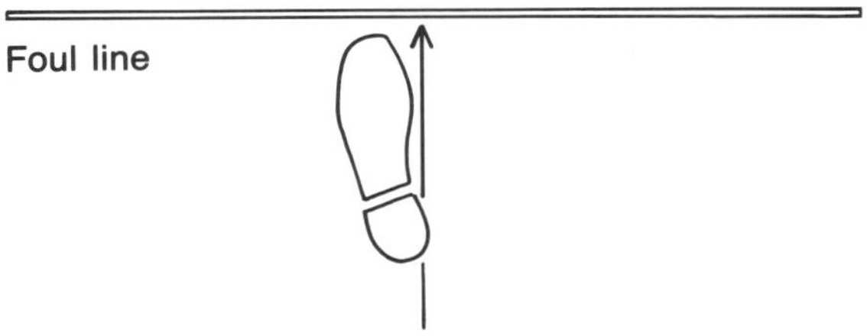

- Sliding foot turned slightly away from swing
- Hips probably perpendicular to swing
- Ball timed with swing

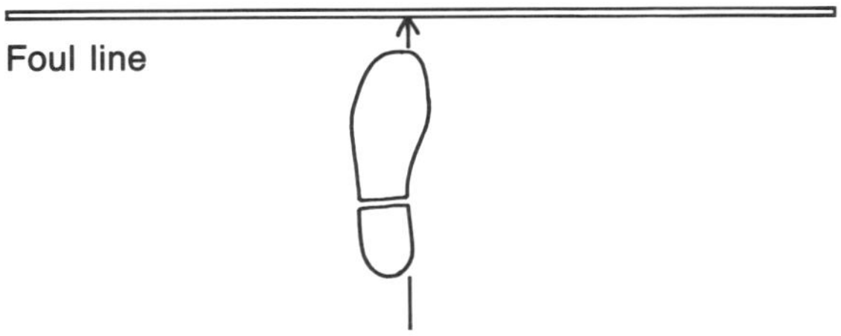

- Sliding foot turned slightly toward swing
- Hips and shoulders turned away from swing
- Ball slightly later than foot in slide

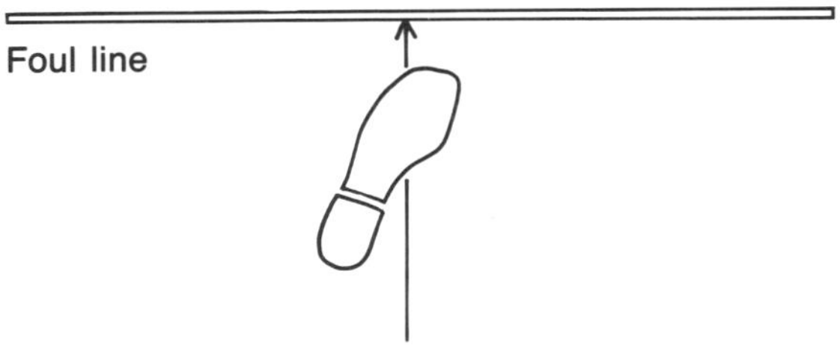

- Sliding foot turned greatly toward swing
- Hips and shoulders turned greatly from swing
- Ball much later than foot in slide

Instructions to Class

- "Ask your partner to observe you as you bowl 30 frames, rating you on the characteristics listed in your book."
- "Partners, because it is easy to observe more than one characteristic at a time, you may select two or three characteristics to observe at one time."
- "Alternate bowling a frame with observing your partner for a frame."

Student Option

- "Bowl two games to give your partner more observation time."

Student Success Goal

- 25 out of 30 possible points

To Decrease Difficulty

- Have partner observe one characteristic at a time.
- Have bowler repeat drill alone.

To Increase Difficulty

- Have partners compare rating results while bowling two games.

3. *Bowl for Score*

[Corresponds to *Bowling*, Step 13, Drill 3]

Group Management and Safety Tips

- This drill works well with or without partner's evaluation.
- Encourage experimentation of walking in the direction of the pins to pick up spares.
- Encourage proper courtesy as well as accurate scoring.

Instructions to Class

- "The purposes of this drill are to execute a coordinated finished delivery that represents your best technique, to practice scoring a game, to use strike-targeting techniques, and to start picking up your spares."
- "Alternate bowling one frame with your partner for a complete game. Tally the number of pins knocked down for both balls. To pick up spares at this point, set up as normal, move your setup location directly opposite the remaining pins, and experiment with walking in the direction of the remaining pins."

Student Options

- ''Ask your partner to evaluate your technique according to the Coordinated Finished Delivery Keys to Success Checklist in your book.''
- ''Bowl two games by scoring the actual pins knocked down only for your first-ball delivery. For your second-ball delivery, score either a spare or a miss, depending upon your technique execution of a mutually agreed upon aspect, for example, a smooth, coordinated full delivery, or a proper finish, or hitting your target, and so forth. Select an aspect you most need to work on.''

Student Success Goal

- Bowl a game

To Decrease Difficulty

- Have students score only first-ball delivery results. They will need to bowl two games to complete one game line on their scoresheet. The second-ball delivery can be used to practice strike-targeting.

To Increase Difficulty

- Have students score two games.

4. *Varied Step-Number Delivery*

[New drill]

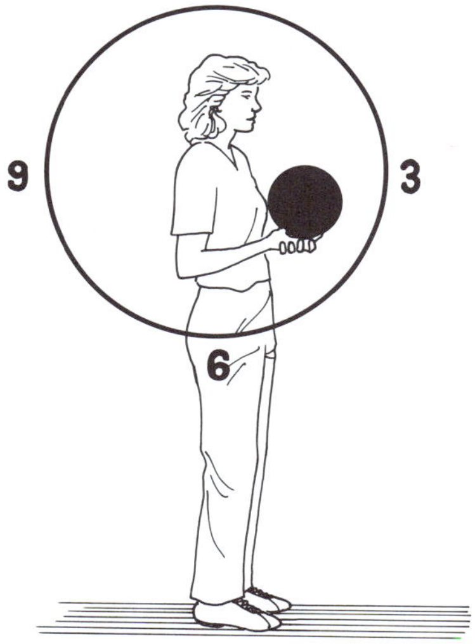

Group Management and Safety Tips

- The instructions and demonstration for this drill are best given to an individual or a small group.
- This is an optional drill that can be used as a learning ''bonus'' for advanced or highly motivated students. The rationale is that a bowler with a clear concept of the four-step delivery should be able to deliver the ball taking any number of steps from one to five, yet preserve the free-pendulum nature of the swing. Furthermore, the ability to take any number of steps may help correct persistent timing problems in the most common four-step delivery.
- You may want to make a poster or handout of the following chart:

Number of steps	Position of ball as first step begins	Foot taking first step
1	9 o'clock	Balance-side
2	6 o'clock	Swingside
3	3 o'clock	Balance-side
4	Setup	Swingside
5	Setup	Balance-side

Instructions and Cues to Individual or Small Groups

- ''It is possible to deliver the ball taking any number of steps from one to five, yet preserve the free-pendulum nature of your swing. If you can successfully deliver the ball in proper time while taking any number of steps, you may later be able to isolate, identify, and correct timing problems in your usual delivery. Some of you, who want to start off with your balance-side foot, may prefer the five-step approach. Most of you will find that the four-step approach works best because the ball and the first step move together. The variations help illustrate technique errors. For example, if your partner observes that you are bending too far forward on your second step, switch to a three-step approach to feel the full results of this error.''
- ''You already know how to execute the one-step and four-step deliveries.''
- ''A two-step delivery is the least common. First step on your swingside foot with the ball at a 6 o'clock arm-extended position.''
- ''A three-step delivery starts on the balance-side foot with the ball at a 3 o'clock arm-extended position.''
- ''A five-step delivery starts on the balance-side foot with the ball at setup position.''

Student Option

- ''You decide how many deliveries you need to feel comfortable.''

Student Success Goal

- Demonstrate correct timing of the pendulum swing and the selected number of steps

To Decrease Difficulty

- Let the student not use a ball.

To Increase Difficulty

- Not applicable.

Step 14 Spare Targeting

Spare targeting is identical to strike targeting, with one exception: the desired pin impact point changes with each spare leave. This may require an adjustment of either the setup location, the target, or both.

The advantage of skilled spare-making is that a bowler can avoid really low game averages. It is possible to average 190 even if students never get a strike. Spare *leaves* provide variety in bowling; they are opportunities to become more accurate and versatile. The student who remembers the following simple rules and some board numbers will become a superior spare bowler.

1. If the spare leave is to the inside (the balance side), move the setup location to the outside (the swingside); if it is outside, move to the inside.
2. Always walk toward the spare leave.
3. Always choose a *spare impact point* that allows the spare ball to hit the pin closest to the bowler first.
4. Always choose a spare impact point that allows the ball to contact the most pins.
5. Always *translate* any spare leave into a simpler one before deciding on how to shoot it.
6. After translating the spare leave, fit to it one of the seven spare target lines detailed in the drills. Then make appropriate adjustments of your target line and setup location relative to the original strike target line.

Spare-targeting effectiveness cannot be mastered within a single course; the skills take months—even years—to develop. Consequently, your students will show a very wide range of abilities. You should practice watching bowlers roll their balls at various spare leaves, paying close attention to the ball paths. This will help you develop the sharp eye necessary for observing differences among your students' performances.

STUDENT KEYS TO SUCCESS

- Recognize spare leave
- Translate spare leave
- Choose target point and touchdown point
- Take appropriate setup location
- Turn feet parallel with target line
- Focus eyes on visual target
- Execute well
- Analyze results
- Adjust target line if necessary
- Repeat execution

Spare Targeting Rating		
CRITERION	**BEGINNING LEVEL**	**ACCOMPLISHED LEVEL**
Knowledge of Rules	• No concept	• Can recite all
Target Line	• No concept	• Clear choice for particular spare leave
Setup Location	• No concept	• Appropriate for chosen target line
Angle of Feet to Target Line	• No concept	• Parallel with target line and approach line
Visual Target	• Inappropriate for given spare leave	• Appropriate for the spare leave, and to compensate for any visual error
Target Line Adjustment	• No concept	• Usually appropriate in response to previous delivery

Error Detection and Correction for Spare Targeting

If students strictly adhere to the principles of good spare-making before stepping up onto the approach to attempt a spare, they will be taking a significant step toward minimizing spare-targeting errors. If they do not, they may attempt to *shoot* spares with a poorly selected target line, thereby missing many spares even before rolling the ball. Any errors that occur after a bowler has chosen the correct spare impact point and a correct target line would be identical with those for strike targeting.

Refer to the ''Error Detection and Correction'' section of Step 6 for applicable information; simply substitute the words *spare* for *strike*, and *spare impact point* for *pocket* or *strike pocket* in the examples. The best position for observing the results of spare attempts is from the back and to the swingside.

Spare Targeting Drills

1. *Pocket Spares*

[Corresponds to *Bowling,* Step 14, Drill 1]

Sample Scoresheet

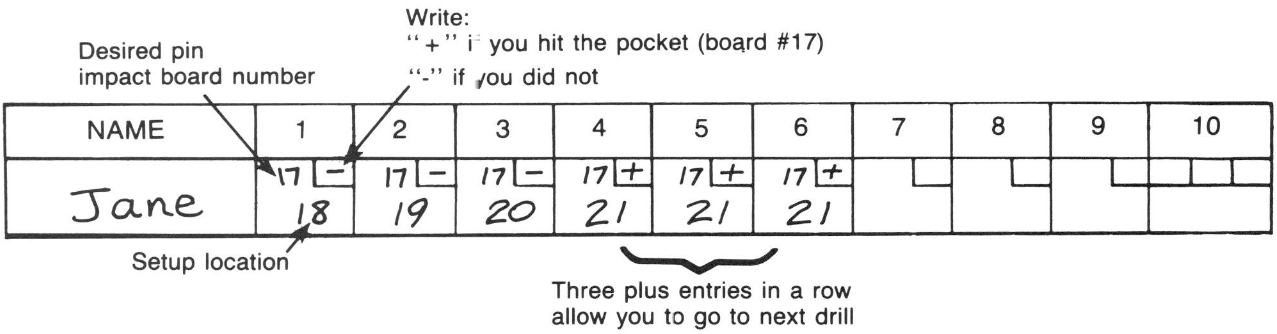

Group Management and Safety Tip

- One or more bowlers work per lane, taking turns bowling at full racks of pins, disregarding pin reaction.

Instructions to Class

- "Prepare a scoresheet like the Sample Scoresheet in your book."
- "Deliver your ball at a full rack of pins. If you hit the pocket squarely, put a '+' in the small box in the upper right corner of the appropriate frame on your scoresheet. If you didn't hit the pocket squarely, enter a '–.' If you did not execute well or you did not hit your spare target line, do not record anything."
- "Make 1-board adjustments to your setup location if necessary. Record the new setup location in the appropriate frame. In your book, in the space marked 'Your Score,' write the board number where you set up when you were the most accurate."
- "Repeat this drill until you hit the pocket three times in succession with proper execution."
- "Keep your approach line parallel with your target line—not necessarily perpendicular to the foul line—as you shift your target line diagonally across the lane."

Student Option

- "Ask your partner to give you feedback on how accurately you hit the pocket."

Student Success Goals

- Identify your most accurate setup location
- Hit the selected spare impact point 3 times in 3 attempts

To Decrease Difficulty

- Let student hit the selected spare impact point 2 times in 3 attempts.

To Increase Difficulty

- Have student hit the selected spare impact point 5 out of 5 attempts.

2. *Near-Inside (Balance Side) Spares*

[Corresponds to *Bowling*, Step 14, Drill 2]

Group Management and Safety Tip

- One or more bowlers work per lane, taking turns bowling at full racks of pins.

Instructions to Class

- ''Repeat the previous drill using the 2 pin (RH) or the 3 pin (LH) as your intended impact pin. Use the second arrow as your target point. Move your feet 4 boards outside your strike setup location.''
- ''Keep score as before, giving yourself a '+' for a square hit on the impact pin and a '−' for any other hit.''

Student Option

- ''Ask your partner to give you feedback on the accuracy of hitting your target point and intended impact pin.''

Student Success Goals

- Identify your most accurate setup location
- Hit the selected spare impact point 3 times in 3 attempts

To Decrease Difficulty

- Let student hit the selected spare impact point 2 times in 3 attempts.

To Increase Difficulty

- Have student hit the selected spare impact point 5 out of 5 times.

3. *Medium-Inside (Balance Side) Spares*

[Corresponds to *Bowling*, Step 14, Drill 3]

Group Management and Safety Tip

- One or more bowlers work per lane, taking turns bowling at full racks of pins.

Instructions to Class

- ''Repeat the previous drill using the 4 pin (RH) or the 6 pin (LH) as your intended impact pin, and the second arrow as your target point.''
- ''Move your setup location 8 boards to the outside.''

Student Option

- ''Ask your partner to give you feedback on the accuracy of hitting your target point and intended impact pin.''

Student Success Goals

- Identify your most accurate setup location
- Hit the selected spare impact point 3 times in 3 attempts

To Decrease Difficulty

- Let student hit the selected spare impact point 2 times in 3 attempts.

To Increase Difficulty

- Have student hit the selected spare impact point 5 out of 5 times.

4. *Far-Inside (Balance Side) Corner Pin Spares*

[Corresponds to *Bowling*, Step 14, Drill 4]

Group Management and Safety Tip

- One or more bowlers work per lane, taking turns bowling at full racks of pins.

Instructions to Class

- "Repeat the previous drill using the 7 pin (RH) or the 10 pin (LH) as your intended impact pin, and the second arrow as your target point."
- "Move your setup location 12 boards to the outside."

Student Option

- "Ask your partner to give you feedback on the accuracy of hitting your target point and intended impact pin."

Student Success Goals

- Identify your most accurate setup location
- Hit the selected spare impact point 3 times in 3 attempts

To Decrease Difficulty

- Let student hit the selected spare impact point 2 times in 3 attempts.

To Increase Difficulty

- Have student hit the selected spare impact point 5 out of 5 times.

5. *Near-Outside (Swingside) Spares*

[Corresponds to *Bowling*, Step 14, Drill 5]

Group Management and Safety Tip

- One or more bowlers work per lane, taking turns bowling at full racks of pins.

Instructions to Class

- "Repeat the previous drill using the 3 pin (RH) or the 2 pin (LH) as your intended impact point, and the third arrow as your target point."
- "Move your setup location 7 boards to the inside."

Student Option

- "Ask your partner to give you feedback on the accuracy of hitting your target point and intended impact pin."

Student Success Goals

- Identify your most accurate setup location
- Hit the selected spare impact point 3 times in 3 attempts

To Decrease Difficulty

- Let student hit the selected spare impact point 2 times in 3 attempts.

To Increase Difficulty

- Have student hit the selected spare impact point 5 out of 5 times.

6. *Medium-Outside (Swingside) Spares*

[Corresponds to *Bowling*, Step 14, Drill 6]

Group Management and Safety Tip

- One or more bowlers work per lane, taking turns bowling at full racks of pins.

Instructions to Class

- ''Repeat the previous drill using the 6 pin (RH) or the 4 pin (LH) as your intended impact pin, and the third arrow as your target point.''
- ''Move your setup location 11 boards to the inside.''

Student Option

- ''Ask your partner to give you feedback on the accuracy of hitting your target point and intended impact pin.''

Student Success Goals

- Identify your most accurate setup location
- Hit the selected spare impact point 3 times in 3 attempts

To Decrease Difficulty

- Let student hit the selected spare impact point 2 times in 3 attempts.

To Increase Difficulty

- Have student hit the selected spare impact point 5 out of 5 times.

7. *Far-Outside (Swingside) Corner Pin Spares*

[Corresponds to *Bowling*, Step 14, Drill 7]

Group Management and Safety Tip

- One or more bowlers working per lane, taking turns bowling at full racks of pins.

Instructions to Class

- ''Repeat the previous drill using the 10 pin (RH) or the 7 pin (LH) as your intended impact pin, and the third arrow as your target point.''
- ''Move your setup location 13 boards to the inside.''

Student Option

- ''Ask your partner to give you feedback on the accuracy of hitting your target point and intended impact pin.''

Student Success Goals

- Identify your most accurate setup location
- Hit the selected spare impact point 3 times in 3 attempts

To Decrease Difficulty

- Let student hit the selected spare impact point 2 times in 3 attempts.

To Increase Difficulty

- Have student hit the selected spare impact point 5 out of 5 times.

8. *Spare Cleanup*

[Corresponds to *Bowling*, Step 14, Drill 8]

Group Management and Safety Tip

- Two persons bowl per lane, alternately rolling the first ball and the second ball.

Instructions to Class

- ''Bowl three games with a partner. In the first frame of the first game, your partner will roll the first ball, practicing good strike-targeting technique. You attempt to pick up any pins left.''
- ''In the second frame, reverse roles so that you roll the first ball and let your partner convert the spare.''
- ''Continue alternating throughout the three games.''

Student Option

- ''Decide rotation order with your partner, dependent upon each other's goals, for example, improving strike-targeting techniques, practicing spares at a full rack of pins, adapting to a variety of multiple-pin spare leaves, and so forth.''

Student Success Goal

- 80% spare conversion in any single game

To Decrease Difficulty

- Not applicable.

To Increase Difficulty

- Not applicable.

9. *Corner Pin Sharpshooter*

[Corresponds to *Bowling*, Step 14, Drill 9]

Group Management and Safety Tip

- Two or more persons bowl per lane, or pair of lanes.

Instructions to Class

- ''This drill involves a high degree of spare-shooting accuracy and some competition.''
- ''Keep your score on a regular scoresheet, but write only points—not strikes and spares—in the frames. The objective is to outscore your opponent while attempting to get a perfect score of 200 (only two balls allowed in the 10th frame).''
- ''Try to knock down only the 7 pin and the 10 pin. Give yourself 10 points per pin if you knock these pins down.''
- ''If you knock the 4-7-8 or the 6-9-10 pins down, give yourself 5 points per cluster. If you knock down any other pin or pins, your score is zero for the *frame*. Any balls rolled into the channel are worth − 20 points.''

Student Option

- ''You can play this game in competition against one opponent, or you can team up with a partner and bowl against two opponents, adding your two games to get one doubles team score.''

Student Success Goal

- Outscore your opponent with as high a score as you can bowl (200 points maximum)

To Decrease Difficulty

- Let student bowl for a personal best score out of the three games.

To Increase Difficulty

- Let student create own points per pin system.

10. *Call Shot Game*

[Corresponds to *Bowling*, Step 14, Drill 10]

Group Management and Safety Tip

- Two or more persons bowl per lane, or pair of lanes.

Instructions to Class

- "Before you roll your first ball, declare how many pins you will leave standing. If you leave standing the *exact* number of pins you declared, you get 10 points. If you leave any other number of pins standing, your opponent gets 10 points. If you declare and make a strike, you get 30 points. Any time you roll the ball into the channel, your opponent gets 5 points."
- "Your opponent must try to convert your spare. If successful, your opponent gets 5 points; if not, you get 5 points."
- "Each frame, you and your opponent alternate rolling the first ball."
- "On separate game lines of a scoresheet, keep track of the points—not strikes or spares—that you and your opponent get."

Student Option

- "You may bowl against a single opponent or pair up for doubles."

Student Success Goal

- Outscore your opponent with as high a score as you can bowl

To Decrease Difficulty

- Let student bowl without an opponent.

To Increase Difficulty

- Let student bowl two or more games using this declared pin and point system.

11. *Battle*

[Corresponds to *Bowling*, Step 14, Drill 11]

Group Management and Safety Tip

- Two teams—each made of two or more bowlers, depending on the size of the class—compete against each other on a pair of lanes.

Instructions to Class

- "In this game, everyone on your team is competing against the opposing team. The team on the odd-numbered lane bowls first."
- "The leadoff bowler on the odd lane tries to get more pins than he or she thinks the leadoff bowler on the even lane can get."
- "The leadoff bowler on the even lane tries to match or better the opponent's first-ball pinfall. If there is at least a match, then the even-lane team adds 20 bonus points to their score. If there is no match or betterment of pinfall, then the odd-lane team gets the 20 bonus points."
- "Each bowler attempts to convert his or her spares, and keeps regular score throughout the game."
- "In the second frame, the second bowler from the even-lane team goes first. Continue alternating both team and team member order throughout the game."
- "With 12 balls possible in a 10-frame game, there are 240 bonus points at stake."

Student Option

- "You may battle for double bonus points by matching or bettering both the first and the second ball of each frame. An unmatched strike on the first ball automatically earns 40 bonus points."

Student Success Goal

- Complete 2 games of Battle, bowling the higher team point total

To Decrease Difficulty

- Let students bowl only for pins.
- Use a possible 10 bonus points per first ball of a frame.

To Increase Difficulty

- Match students of equal ability in the team lineups.

12. *Bowling Bingo*

[Corresponds to *Bowling*, Step 14, Drill 12]

Sample Scoresheet for Bingo

2-4	5-8	9-12	13-16	17-20
2	Free	10	14	20
4	7	12	16	Free
2	6	Free	15	17
Free	5	9	13	18
3	8	11	Free	19

Group Management and Safety Tips

- This game allows total class participation.
- Depending on the size of the class, two teams of two or more bowlers may bowl on a pair of lanes. Then, these two teams may join forces to compete against all other paired teams. Each team uses one Bowling Bingo card per game.
- Warn your students not to race. Bowling should proceed at the usual pace, and normal lane courtesy should be observed.
- Since this drill uses only first-ball pinfall, you could have some team members working on spare targeting (instead of resetting the pins), and having two different bingo games per team (for first-ball pinfalls and for second-ball pinfalls).

Equipment

- Bingo cards, 1 per team per game (use a regular scoresheet and divide it into 5 by 5 grids)

Instructions to Class

- "Bowlers on lanes 1 and 2 are pair 1; those on lanes 3 and 4 are pair 2, and so forth. Each pair uses one Bowling Bingo card per game."
- "The numbers in the 25 Bowling Bingo squares range from 2 to 20. Only one number on a card may be crossed out per two-bowler attempt."
- "The two leadoff bowlers of each pair add together only their first-ball pinfall, and mark off the appropriate total number on their Bingo cards. Then, reset the pins."
- "The second bowlers of each pair do the same, and so on. Only one first ball is bowled in the 10th frame. The first pair to 'Bingo' wins the game."

Student Option

- "Create your own Bowling Bingo card by either scrambling the numbers within a vertical column, or using a unique pattern (see Example Bingo Patterns in your book) for winning 'Bingo.'"

Student Success Goal

- Bowl 2 games of Bowling Bingo

To Decrease Difficulty

- Bowl 1 game of Bowling Bingo.

To Increase Difficulty

- Have leadoff pairs count combined first-ball pinfalls, then the second bowlers of each pair count combined second-ball pinfalls, and so on. If no pins are hit, a pair loses a turn.

13. *Cutthroat Crossover*

[Corresponds to *Bowling*, Step 14, Drill 13]

Group Management and Safety Tips

- Two teams—each of two or more bowlers, depending on the size of the class—compete against each other on a pair of lanes.
- Unlike regulation team competition, all bowlers on a team participate together in bowling only a single game line. The game line on the odd lane is the score for the odd team, and the game line on the even lane is the score for the even team.

Instructions to Class

- ''All members of one team bowl a single game against the other team.''
- ''The leadoff person for the even team bowls the first ball for the leadoff person on the odd team, and vice versa. Each bowler then attempts to convert his or her *own* spare. If the first ball goes in the channel, it is a strike for the bowler's opponents.''
- ''Repeat this process throughout the entire game, with the second bowler from each team bowling the first ball of the other team's second frame score, and so forth.''

Student Option

- ''You may use this drill for singles competition.''

Student Success Goal

- Play and win 2 games of Cutthroat Crossover

To Decrease Difficulty

- Not applicable.

To Increase Difficulty

- Not applicable.

14. *Half-Pyramid*

[Corresponds to *Bowling*, Step 14, Drill 14]

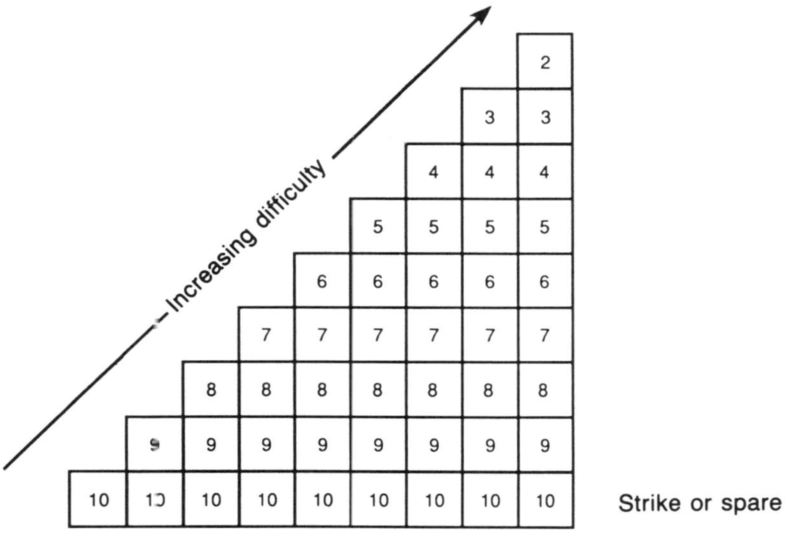

Group Management and Safety Tips

- Competition is between two teams on a pair of lanes.
- If necessary, standing pins may be swept off the pin deck.

Instructions to Class

- "This is a fun accuracy game that requires spare-targeting ability."
- "The objective is to cross out a half-pyramid of numbers on a specially prepared scoresheet by matching the numbers with first- and second-ball pin count. Note the scoresheet example, and begin at the bottom of the pyramid and work upward. If your total pinfall matches the number, mark it off. Try to cross out all your numbers before your opponents cross out theirs."

Student Option

- "You may adjust the Success Goal to better fit your needs, for example, achieving a certain line or number(s) per line."

Student Success Goal

- Complete 2 games of Half-Pyramid, attempting to cross out all numbers before the opposing team

To Decrease Difficulty

- Reduce the Success Goal.

To Increase Difficulty

- Let student start higher on the half-pyramid.

15. *Tic-Tac-Bowl*

[Corresponds to *Bowling*, Step 14, Drill 15]

Group Management and Safety Tip

- On a pair of lanes, either individuals or teams compete against each other.

Instructions to Class

- ''This is a fun accuracy game that requires strike- and spare-targeting abilities.''
- ''The objective is the same as the traditional Tic-Tac-Toe game—to get three X or O entries in a row horizontally, vertically, or diagonally on the game board. The right to place an X or an O on the board is earned by making correct first- and second-ball attempts.''
- ''Toss a coin to decide who starts first, then alternate rolling two balls each, attempting to get a strike. The first player to get either a strike or convert the spare, gets to place his or her mark on the Tic-Tac-Bowl board.''

Student Option

- ''You may design your own ways to earn X and O entries.''

Student Success Goal

- Complete 3 or more games of Tic-Tac-Bowl

To Decrease Difficulty

- Reduce the Success Goal.

To Increase Difficulty

- Increase the criteria to earn an X or O entry.

16. *Bowling Golf*

[Corresponds to *Bowling*, Step 14, Drill 16]

Group Management and Safety Tip

- Competition is held on either a single lane or a pair of lanes. If there are less than three persons assigned to a lane, the bowlers on a pair of lanes play against each other and alternate lanes. If more than three, bowlers on a lane compete among themselves on their single lane.''

Instructions to Class

- ''This drill combines the golf concept of shooting par with strike and spare skills. Ten 'holes,' or frames, constitute a round of Bowling Golf. Each 'golfer,' or bowler, uses a single regulation bowling game line but does not keep a regulation bowling score. Note the scoring and rules of play in your text.''

Student Option

- ''Here's a skins game variation: Award 5 points to the winner of an individual hole (frame). In case of a tie for hole winner, carry over the 5 points, adding them to the winner's points on the next hole.''

Student Success Goals

- Complete 1 round of Bowling Golf, attempting to make the lowest score
- Skins game: Complete 1 round of golf, attempting to accumulate the greatest number of points

To Decrease Difficulty

- Not applicable.

To Increase Difficulty

- Not applicable.

Step 15 Goal Setting

Effective goal setting, or success management by objectives, incorporates the following principles:

- *Set challenging but realistic goals*—A performer should set high standards but should be able to reach them. Be prepared to help students recognize their limits.
- *Set performance goals*—A performer should specify what type of result is desired in terms of performance goals, which focus on execution, rather than in terms of outcome goals, such as expected pinfall or wins. Performance goals place the emphasis on the performer instead of fate, thereby placing responsibility for success and control in the hands of the performer.
- *Set some short-range goals*—In order not to lose enthusiasm, a performer should designate some goals as stepping stones to the attainment of long-range goals. These short-range goals act as feedback along the way to ultimate-goal attainment.
- *Set specifically stated goals*—The wording used for goals is important. Any goal should very specifically state what is desired in terms of performance.
- *Set only positive-action goals*—Goals should be in the active voice to be most effective. An example of an effective goal is "I will hit my target squarely five times."

Students will probably catch on quickly to goal setting. The most blatant goal-setting error is that of not setting any goals! Next in severity would be setting nonspecific goals. No errors are discussed in this section; see "How to Set Goals" in the participant's book.

STUDENT KEYS TO SUCCESS

- Set realistic performance goals
- Set short-range goals
- Set long-range goals
- Set specifically stated goals
- Set positive-action goals
- Show performance-oriented behavior

Goal-Setting Drills

1. *Goal Development*

[Corresponds to *Bowling*, Step 15, Drill 1]

Group Management and Safety Tips

- Two persons, working together.
- Some members of the class may want to repeat past drills that they feel would help achieve their goals.

Equipment

- Pencils and paper for everyone

Instructions to Class

- "Working with a partner, pick one or more goals from the 'Sample List of Ultimate Goals' in your book. Write down your selection(s), and under each, write the short-range goals or strategies you will use to attain the goal."

- "Draw a flowchart like the one in Figure 15.1 in your book [see following Figure 15.1a, b, c]. Discuss the realism of your goals with your partner. Check that you have stated performance versus outcome goals."

Student Option

- "You may create a drill that would help you achieve one of your goals."

Student Success Goal

- Develop one or more ultimate goals that are positive, written in an active voice, and performance-oriented

To Decrease Difficulty

- Not applicable.

To Increase Difficulty

- Not applicable.

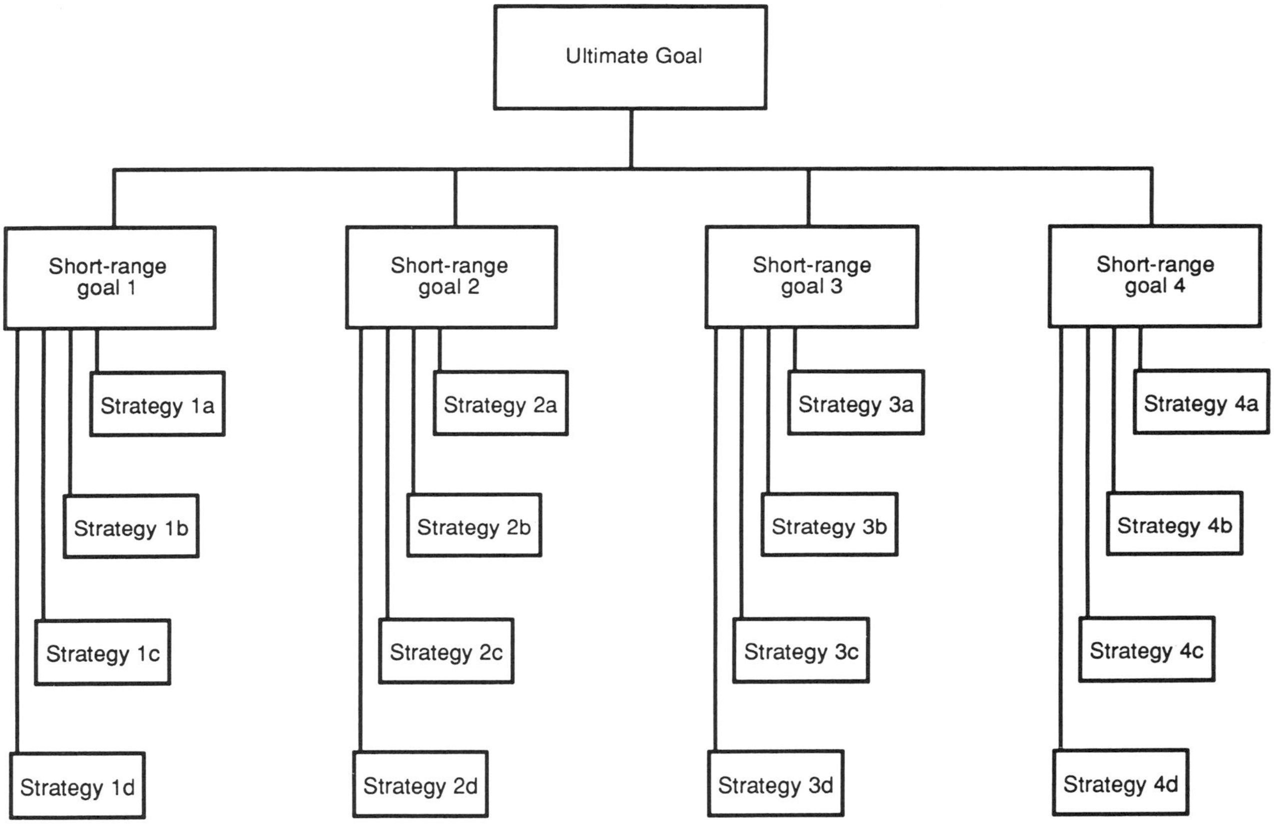

a

(Cont.)

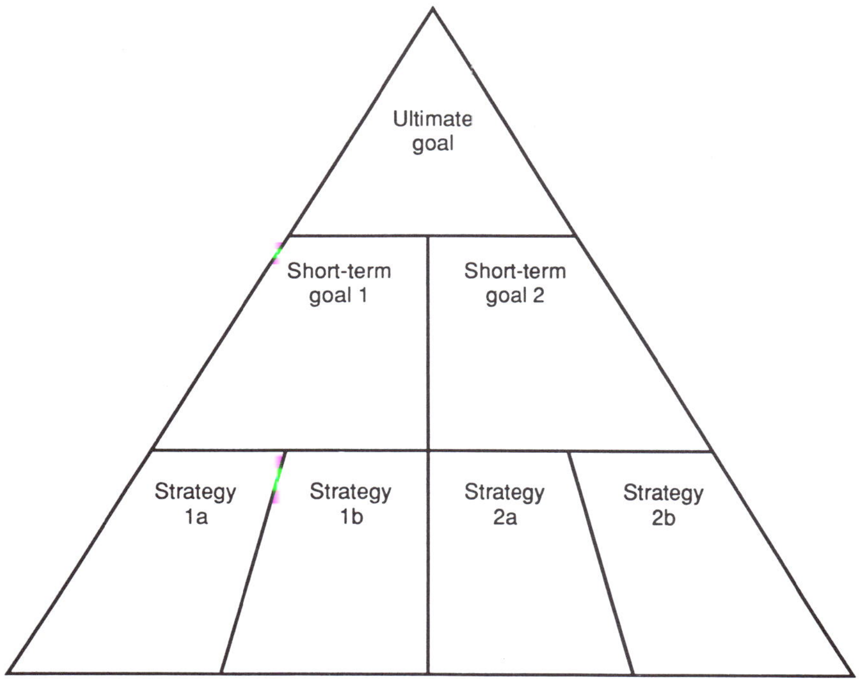

b

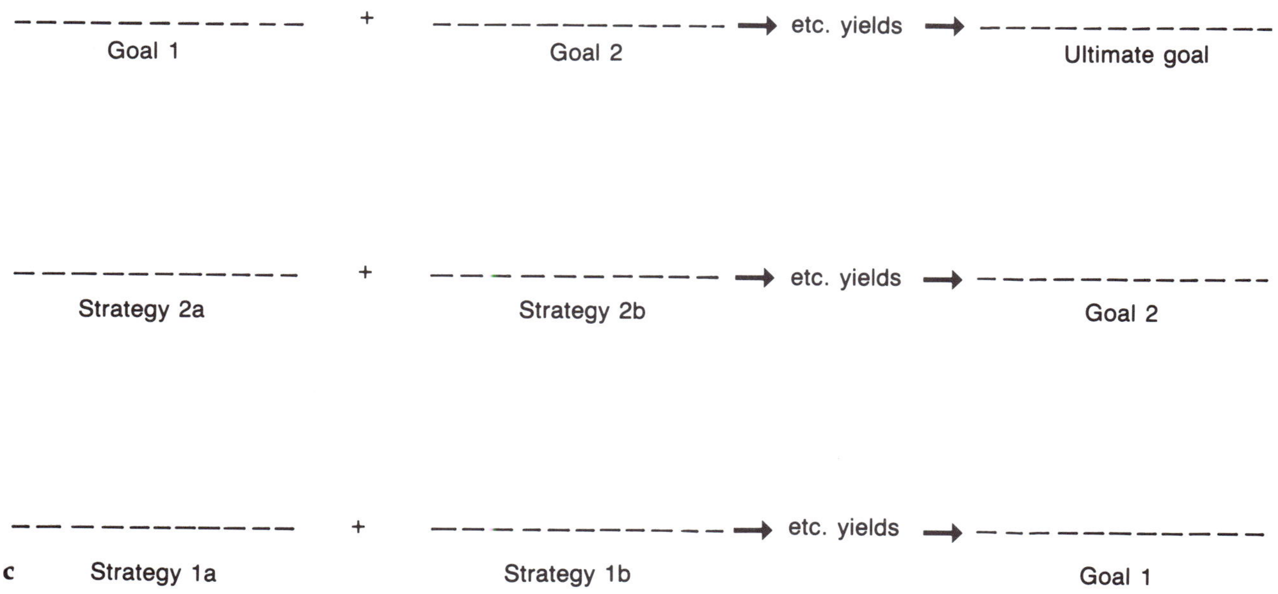

c

Figure 15.1a, b, c Three different types of flowcharts for goal setting.

2. *Personal Goal Development*

[Corresponds to *Bowling*, Step 15, Drill 2]

Group Management and Safety Tips

- This is a solo drill.
- Other members of the class may repeat useful past drills while their lane mates are working on goal development. See the examples in the previous drill.

Equipment

- Pencils for everyone
- Paper, 10 sheets per student

Instructions to Class

- "Write down 10 of your own ultimate goals in your book. Then transfer each goal to its own sheet of paper."
- "Develop at least two of your goals as you did in the previous drill. Set challenging but attainable performance goals."
- "Share these with me, then finish developing the remaining eight goals on your own."

Student Option

- "You may jointly develop goals with a partner."

Student Success Goal

- Develop 10 personal goals

To Decrease Difficulty

- Have student develop only one or two goals.

To Increase Difficulty

- Have students identify past drills or create drills that will help them achieve one or more of their goals.

3. *Short-Range Goals*

[Corresponds to *Bowling*, Step 15, Drill 3]

Group Management and Safety Tip

- This is a solo drill.
- Some members of the class may want to repeat past drills that they feel would help achieve their goals.

Equipment

- Pencils for everyone
- Paper, 5 sheets per student

Instructions to Class

- "In the proper space in your book, write down five short-range goals that you hope to achieve during a game."
- "Bowl two games and record whether or not you achieved these goals."
- "Evaluate and modify your short-range goals as necessary for you to be able to achieve them."

Student Option

- "You may jointly develop short-range goals with a partner."

Student Success Goal

- Develop and achieve 5 short-range goals

To Decrease Difficulty

- Have students develop one or two short-range goals.

To Increase Difficulty

- Have students identify past drills or create drills that will help them achieve one or more of their goals.
- Let students plan an hour-long practice session.

Step 16 Practicing for Success

Practice is important because it potentially improves performance. Practice can be fascinating when positive, visible change takes place in a player's performance. Students should be made to understand that practice sessions are mirrors to success, providing frequent opportunities to see themselves accomplishing short-range goals that lead to long-range improvements.

The two general types of practice, physical and mental, are discussed below. Three types of physical practice are distinguished: *unsupervised*, or *solo*, practice; *reciprocal*, or *buddy system*, practice; and *supervised*, or *instructional*, practice. There is only one type of mental practice here: mental imagery, or mental rehearsal. Persons who want to derive the most benefit from practice should engage in all of the following:

- *Unsupervised (solo) practice*—Practice in solitude is important for learning new movements that require thoughtful repetition.
- *Reciprocal (buddy system) practice*—Practice with a partner provides the performer a way of obtaining accurate, instantaneous feedback from an observer.
- *Supervised (instructional) practice*—Practice with a trained supervisor or teacher is beneficial because it focuses on the basics, the fundamentals.
- *Mental practice*—Detailed, imagined rehearsal of movement helps a performer ingrain correct movements into muscle memory without actually bowling.

The foremost practice errors are (a) the outright absence of practice and (b) casual bowling without objectives. No errors will be discussed in this section. As necessary, refer students to the "How to Set Goals" section in Step 15 of the participant's book.

STUDENT KEYS TO SUCCESS

- Set aside practice time
- Select quiet environment
- Use preset practice goals
- Use four practice types
- Evaluate self constantly
- Adjust goals when necessary

Practice Drills

1. Charting Progress: Unsupervised Practice

[Corresponds to *Bowling*, Step 16, Drill 1]

Sample Self-Scorecard

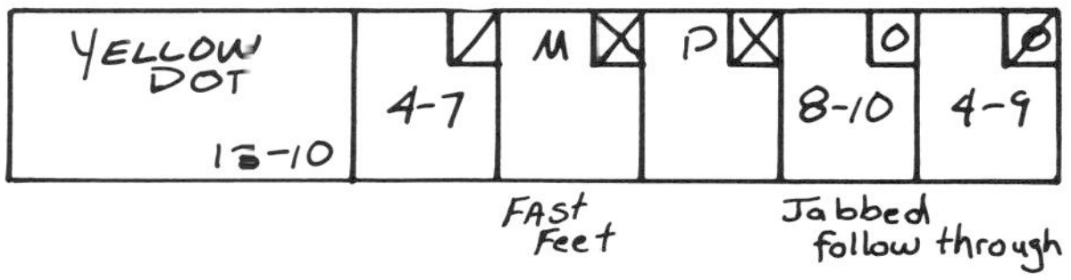

Group Management and Safety Tips

- One person bowls per lane.
- It is difficult to use this drill in a group setting because the bowler needs to make consecutive shots at a quick pace without waiting for others to bowl in between. Thus, you may want to designate one or more pairs of lanes at one end for this drill, while the rest of the class does Drills 2 and 3. Or, you may want to assign this drill for an outside of class assignment, especially if you have a very large class.

Instructions to Class

- ''Not only should you attempt this and the following solo drills in class, but you should use your practice (open play) time outside of class to accomplish the drills' goals. Solo drills are ideal for anyone practicing on his or her own time.''
- ''This drill shows you how to use a scoresheet to record your performance when practicing alone.''
- ''Record the results of your shots within the frame boxes, and below the respective boxes write in comments regarding your performance. For example, identify the type of strike (see your book), the pins left standing, the ball used, the line played, and so forth. You can learn something about the quality of your approach and delivery in each frame by studying your notations. Such notations may be especially useful in helping you determine skills that need extra attention.''

Student Option

- ''You may complete this drill outside of class.''

Student Success Goal

- Complete and score 1 unsupervised practice game

To Decrease Difficulty

- Not applicable.

To Increase Difficulty

- Not applicable.

2. *Charting Progress: Supervised Practice*

[Corresponds to *Bowling*, Step 16, Drill 2]

Sample Observer Scorecard

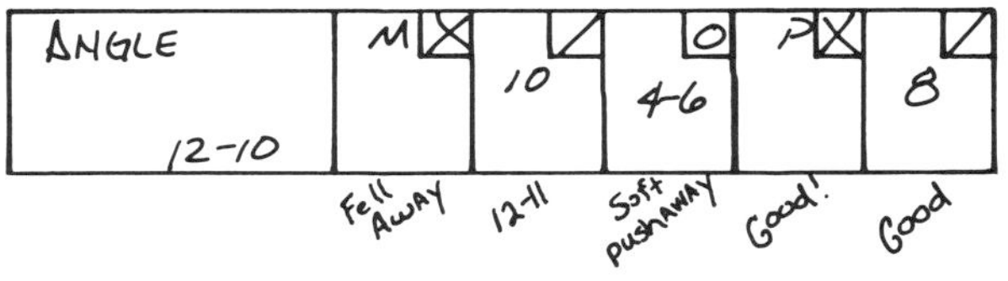

Group Management and Safety Tips

- One person bowls per lane while being observed by another.
- You may want to combine this drill with others that allow more group participation.

Instructions to Class

- ''This drill shows you how to use a scoresheet to record your performance when practicing while being observed by a partner (buddy), an instructor, or a coach. Record the same information relative to your execution and pinfall results that you did in the previous drill.''

- "In addition, your observer can record the actual path that the ball followed; early, late, or in-time pushaway and release; overall posture; and so forth."
- "Such notations help you give attention to skills that you might have neglected due to the difficulty in detecting them on your own."

Student Option

- "You may select which items you want your partner to specifically record on your scoresheet."

Student Success Goal

- Complete 1 supervised practice game

To Decrease Difficulty

- Let student chart only one or two items.

To Increase Difficulty

- Increase the number of items that student charts.

3. *Mental Practice*

[Corresponds to *Bowling*, Step 16, Drill 3]

Group Management and Safety Tips

- One person sits in a quiet, relaxing place, working alone.
- Other members of the class may repeat useful past drills while their lane mates are engaged in mental practice.
- Mental practice may be used between frames, especially if there is a fairly long wait. Remind others not to disturb anyone obviously trying to mentally practice.

Equipment

- Notepad or paper and pencil, 1 each per student

Instructions to Class

- "You may conduct mental practice anytime or anywhere, but it is best conducted in a peaceful setting, for example, in bed before you go to sleep, or at your desk during a study break."

- "Refer to the 'How to Execute Mental Practice' section in your book for detailed directions. Briefly, the general directions are these: Achieve a comfortable position in a quiet place, relax your muscles systematically, and clear your mind. Use deep, abdominal breathing. However, do not allow yourself to go to sleep. Watch a mental 'film' of yourself bowling. Envision only perfect form resulting in successful results. Try to re-create the actual sensations of a normal bowling center environment."

Student Option

- "You may conduct this drill out of class."

Student Success Goal

- Complete a 3-game series of mental practice, and keep score on a notepad

To Decrease Difficulty

- Not applicable.

To Increase Difficulty

- To challenge the student's concentration in a busy environment, have him or her mentally practice in a commercial bowling center while others are involved with league play.
- The student can sharpen concentration further by mentally practicing beside a noisy radio or with other distractions.

4. *Novelty Doubles Practice*

[New drill]

Group Management and Safety Tips

- Two doubles teams bowl each other on a pair of lanes, alternating lanes each frame as in conventional league play.
- Partners should watch each other as much as possible and give technique and targeting feedback.

Instructions to Class

- "The purpose of this drill is to acquaint you with two variations of reciprocal practice."
- "*Scotch Doubles* is a game in which two persons alternate deliveries in bowling a single regulation game line. Opposing Scotch Doubles teams bowl each other on a pair of lanes, alternating lanes each frame. The leadoff bowler bowls the first ball of the first frame, and his or her partner bowls for the spare. In the event that the leadoff bowler strikes, the partner becomes the leadoff bowler in the next frame. Frame leadoff honors change every time a strike is rolled."
- "*Best Ball Doubles* is slightly different. Again, two persons bowl a single regulation game line, but both partners get up to bowl at the same time, each on one lane of the pair. Partners alternate the lanes on which they bowl each frame. In each frame, the partner on the left lane of the pair (leadoff bowler) bowls first; while the other partner (anchor bowler) waits. If the leadoff bowler rolls a strike, both partners sit down, allowing the other team to bowl. The strike is scored in the appropriate frame of their game line."
- "If the leadoff partner does not strike, the anchor partner has a chance to roll a better pincount for score. If the anchor bowler knocks down more pins *without a more difficult spare*, then the anchor bowler finishes the frame, and the score for that frame is posted."
- "If partners match pincount, they will discuss their options, usually electing the partner with the less difficult spare to roll for score. However, if the anchor bowler has knocked down less pins *with a less difficult spare*, then he or she will probably finish the frame, with that frame's score posted."
- "Remaining pins should be swept off and a full rack of pins set for the opposing team before the second ball attempt."

Student Option

- "You may compete with two or three other teams instead of one other team."

Student Success Goal

- Complete 2 doubles games against opponents, 1 game of Scotch Doubles and 1 of Best Ball Doubles

To Decrease Difficulty

- Not applicable.

To Increase Difficulty

- Not applicable.

5. *Psychological Scorecard*

[New drill]

Group Management and Safety Tip

- This is a solo drill, one person working alone per lane.

Equipment

- Copies of the Mental Toughness routine

Instructions to Class

"A preshot or Mental Toughness routine should begin the instant you walk into the settee area, long before you roll your first ball. It remains in force continuously until after you have rolled your last ball of the competitive session. The objective of a routine is to keep your attention steadily focused on tasks beneficial to your performance and away from thoughts of failure.

"A Mental Toughness routine is not a method of intimidating an opponent; it is neither arrogance nor unfriendliness. It is simply a mental discipline program any performer should use to sustain concentration for superior performance. To create a proper environment for sustained concentration during competition, do these things:

- Maintain mental control during and between games.
- Talk only if it is absolutely necessary; do not initiate or cultivate conversation and do not encourage eye contact.
- *Never* watch anyone bowl. To do so could interfere with your own movement plan, for example, making you speed up your approach or muscle the ball.'

"The phases of the Mental Toughness routine (Figure 16.1), cross-indexed with the flowchart, are as follows:

Relief Time: The preshot portion of your routine takes place in the period of time between shots (usually 2 to 5 minutes) as well as the period between games of a bowling session. Spend this time wisely, using it to plan physical adjustments to lane conditions, to make modifications to your bowling ball, and so on. Sit down and stay calm, isolating yourself from potential interferences. You may assist in keeping score and talk when necessary during relief time, but do not engage in idle conversation.

Mental Planning: Remain seated and focus your thoughts deeply, spending at least 20 seconds preparing yourself before standing up for your next shot (before spare balls or between shots in the 10th frame, you do not have to sit down). During this time, do not keep score or engage in any conversation. Consciously relax your muscles and conduct mental imagery and positive self-talk.

If you are having a problem in achieving good concentration, or if you are bowling on a particularly difficult lane condition, you may expand the mental planning phase to fill the entire time between shots, effectively replacing your relief time. Be aware, however, that you could become mentally fatigued if you do not give yourself sufficient relief time for tension reduction.

Lane Clearance: Take the next-up position you learned in Step 1, holding your ball in your balance arm to minimize strain on your bowling arm. Look at your intended setup location on the approach while you make either different or the same positive self-statements you made during the mental planning phase. Do not let your eyes dwell on the other bowlers. Simply image yourself properly executing the shot (while you simply glance for clearance on either side).

Setup: Right before you initiate movement, add a deep, relaxing breath to your usual setup routine. Make a last positive self-statement and immediately initiate movement.

Automatic Pilot Execution: During practice it may be necessary to focus your attention on your hand, your foot, or the timing between body parts, as you have done in previous steps. However, during competition the fewer things you monitor consciously, the better.

A good suggestion is to always be mindful of your cadence, and of the coordination between your pushaway and your first step, while your gaze is fixed on your visual target. During competition, you should generally be on automatic pilot. However, in the case of predictable lane conditions or slippery or sticky approaches, you may have to carry out additional conscious monitoring of your body parts to ensure some consistency or even your physical safety.

Analysis: Immediately after you have made your shot, objectively analyze it for accuracy, quality of execution, and your mental state. Because performers tend to be very critical of themselves after a poor shot, keeping the mind busy with objective analysis helps to exclude negative feelings. You must be *very analytical for a short period of time*. Then you should enter the relief time phase, using the analysis information and deciding on the strategy for your next shot. Quickly clear your mind and enter the mental planning phase.''

- ''To help you develop and use mental skills to enhance concentration during practice and to reduce pressure during competition, bowl two games strictly following the Mental Toughness routine (Powers, 1986).''
- ''Keep a regular bowling score and, in the game line directly below the one in which you are keeping score, evaluate your mental behaviors according to these abbreviations: N = negative thinking; L = lack of close attention; O = overexcited; U = undermotivated; C = complete mental control; and F = failure to use routine.''
- ''When you are finished, count the frequency of each abbreviation. The most frequent abbreviation indicates your most frequent behavior.''

Student Option

- ''Instead of repeating the Mental Toughness routine exactly, feel free to verbally share with a partner and demonstrate your own mental toughness routine. How does it vary?''

Student Success Goals

- Above-average scores in both games
- Less than two occurrences of each abbreviation besides ''C''
- 20 or more occurrences of abbreviation ''C''

To Decrease Difficulty

- Have students total their tallys after every two frames.

To Increase Difficulty

- With both prior and mutual concensus, one partner may subtly distract the other during game play.

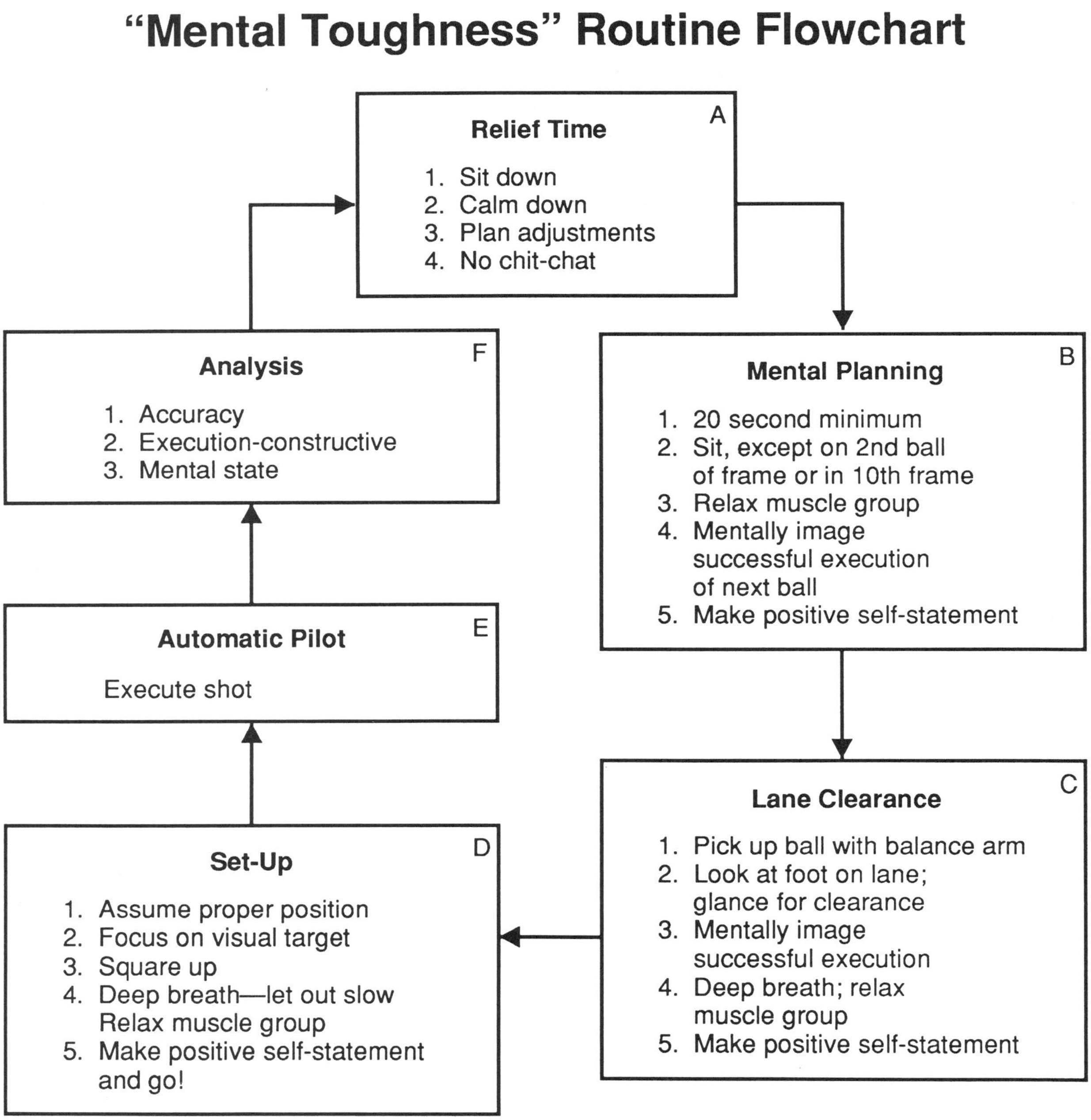
"Mental Toughness" Routine Flowchart
Relief Time
A
1. Sit down
2. Calm down
3. Plan adjustments
4. No chit-chat
Mental Planning
B
1. 20 second minimum
2. Sit, except on 2nd ball of frame or in 10th frame
3. Relax muscle group
4. Mentally image successful execution of next ball
5. Make positive self-statement
Lane Clearance
C
1. Pick up ball with balance arm
2. Look at foot on lane; glance for clearance
3. Mentally image successful execution
4. Deep breath; relax muscle group
5. Make positive self-statement
Set-Up
D
1. Assume proper position
2. Focus on visual target
3. Square up
4. Deep breath—let out slow Relax muscle group
5. Make positive self-statement and go!
Automatic Pilot
E
Execute shot
Analysis
F
1. Accuracy
2. Execution-constructive
3. Mental state

Figure 16.1 The six phases (A-F) of the "Mental Toughness" Routine Flowchart.

Note: Derived from the ideas of W. Powers, personal communication, May, 1987.

Evaluation Ideas

The many special features in the participant's book, *Bowling: Steps to Sucess*, build in an ongoing, daily evaluation system. The Keys to Success list those biomechanical aspects of performance that describe correct body positioning or technique. The Keys to Success Checklists allow qualitative assessments by a trained peer, teacher, or coach of students' technique. The Student Keys to Success in this instructor's guide combines and integrates the numerous, discrete body positions in order to help the learner sequence movements in a fluid manner, which is characteristic of mature performance. The Success Goals in both books are quantitative assessments of your students' performances.

COMBINING QUANTITATIVE AND QUALITATIVE EVALUATION

It is important to combine both performance (quantitative) and technique (qualitative) objectives in your course evaluations in order to satisfy the varying needs and abilities of beginning students. When you combine technique and performance objectives, students who are less skilled or not very experienced will soon learn that they can earn ''A's'' in technique (by following the Keys to Success). This motivates them to practice, and their performance scores tend to improve along with their technique scores. On the other hand, if you evaluate students only in the area of performance, you are creating desperate learners and rewarding only the naturally gifted and the most experienced students taking your beginning course.

AN INDIVIDUAL PROGRAM

A Sample Individual Program is provided (see Appendix C.1) to illustrate evaluation by both technique and performance objectives. A blank individual program sheet is also located in Appendix C.2 for you to fill in your own evaluation system. To best adapt this evaluation system to your specific situation, you need to decide four things: (a) the total number of skills and concepts to assess; (b) the specific criteria to observe; (c) how much weight to place on any one skill or concept, based on the amount of practice time available and the inherent difficulty level [using a multiple of ten with your weighting allows you to enter an item once for ten percent, twice for twenty percent, and so forth]; and (d) the type of grading system to use, for example, letter grades, unsatisfactory or satisfactory, point systems, percentages, merit levels (bronze, silver, gold), and so forth.

Whether or not you emphasize scoring in your evaluation program, consider having students keep score on a regular basis. This will help students learn proper scoring methods. Also, some students tend to perform better if their scores are recorded, even if it is not a score that contributes to their final evaluation. Scoresheets can also be beneficial to you; by examining them after class, you can identify the students who need your special attention during the next session (as well as the ones who didn't attend).

It is recommended that you hand out your evaluation program sheets at your first class meeting. This encourages students to practice and improve, especially if they can assess each other up to a ''B'' grade level, but they must demonstrate for you (and get your initials) for an A-level grade. Providing ongoing testing opportunities avoids a one-chance pressure situation as they get used to performing in front of others, including you. Near the end of your course, you many want to designate a few days as the final testing days in which students can still improve their scores to qualify for an A or top evaluation level. This will prevent your students from trying to increase their performance and technique scores beyond the deadline you set.

ADAPTING INDIVIDUAL PROGRAMS

You are likely to have several students who are either very far behind or very advanced compared to the majority of students. Use the

''To Decrease Difficulty'' and ''To Increase Difficulty'' subsections of all drills to help modify the basic drill directions for these situations. If you find that your students' skill levels divide the class in half, you may want to adjust your individual program for beginning and intermediate students. For example, for the performance objective ''average score after bowling 20 games,'' you might add 10 to 15 points per grade level for intermediate students. Or, halfway through your class, you may want to add an improvement portion to the final grade by comparing the average score of 10 games completed early versus that of 10 later games. However, if students know ahead of time that improvement is part of their grade, they often will ''sandbag.'' Or, you may want to let students decide how much weight they want for each portion of their final grade. Give the students a range of acceptability; for example, no portion of the students' grade may count less than 10 percent or more than 40 percent.

Test Bank

The following questions have been compiled from *Bowling: Steps to Success* for your convenience. Select questions as they fit your needs. Feel free to devise additional, more specific questions in the areas that you would like to emphasize in greater depth.

WRITTEN EXAMINATION QUESTIONS

Directions: Please write the correct letters in the space at the left side of the question number. Each question has one correct answer.

____ 1. Pick up your ball on the ____ only, with ____ , and only after it has come to a stop on the ball return; to avoid mashing your fingers, look at your ball as you pick it up!

a. sides, both hands

b. top, one hand

c. side, one hand

d. top, both hands

____ 2. Bowling can be traced back ____ years to ____ .

a. 500, Germany

b. 7,000, China

c. 2,000, France

d. 7,000, Egypt

____ 3. The ____ Era is characterized by the deemphasis of the sport image of bowling in favor of a recreational image.

a. Competitive

b. Commercial

c. Developmental

d. Club

____ 4. Three common ball fit styles, or grips, are ____ , ____ , and ____ .

a. thumb, middle finger, ring finger

b. spinner, semiroller, full-roller

c. common, unique, stretched

d. conventional, semifingertip, fingertip

____ 5. Before the creation of the All-Star singles match game tournament, the ____ was the means of determining who was the best bowler in the country.

a. ABC Masters

b. U.S. Open

c. Peterson point system

d. challenge match system

____ 6. In bowling, a stable base of support is made possible by high-quality bowling shoes that

a. have a leather sliding sole and a rubber pushing sole.

b. feature the universal sole on both shoes.

c. allow slippage of the pushing foot during the slide.

d. have crepe rubber on both soles and heels.

____ 7. The word *setup* is preferred to *stance* or *address* because it implies that you should
   a. set yourself for a fast push into the delivery.
   b. roll your ball at the rack, or setup, of pins.
   c. systematically set yourself up for decisive movement.
   d. set your feet with the toes pointed at a 45 degree angle.

____ 8. Immediately before stepping up onto the approach, if you stand approximately 2 feet from the end of the approach, holding your ball in your nonbowling arm and looking at the set of dots closest to you, you are in the ____ position.
   a. next-up
   b. setup
   c. cleanup
   d. on deck

____ 9. If you find that your sliding foot is slightly ahead of the other in your setup, you should
   a. reverse your position so your non-sliding foot is slightly ahead.
   b. not be concerned because this is proper positioning.
   c. not be concerned because the placement of the feet does not matter once movement has begun.
   d. place your feet even with each other before movement.

____ 10. By practicing balance awareness drills with your eyes closed, you
   a. focus your attention on the quality of your body balance.
   b. hear your instructor's directions more clearly.
   c. see whether you could find your setup location without looking.
   d. avoid looking at your partner while he or she is observing you.

____ 11. On what three elements should you focus your attention when checking your alignment?
   a. the swingside elbow, the sliding foot, and the second arrow
   b. the swingside shoulder, the ball, and the target
   c. the nonbowling arm, the ball, and the swingside foot
   d. the swingside arm, the sliding foot, and the ball

____ 12. A good safety tip to be followed when you are conducting drills while standing face-to-face with your practice partner is this:

   Swing ____ with the approach. Always check ____ you before swinging a ball. Warn your partner to stop your swinging ball only with his or her ____ on the ____ of the ball.

   a. at an angle, behind, hands, bottom
   b. in line, in front of, fingertips, bottom
   c. at an angle, in front of, fingertips, top
   d. in line, behind, hands, sides

____ 13. If you tend to lose your grip on the ball as it starts into the downswing, the ball is probably ____ and/or ____ .

a. too light, properly fit
b. too heavy, improperly fit
c. too light, improperly fit
d. too heavy, properly fit

____ 14. A ____ is the act of pulling the ball up into the backswing with the muscles of the back of the arm, the shoulder, and the back; it is usually caused by a low, late push-away and a retarded swing.

a. takeaway
b. lever
c. kegel
d. hoist

____ 15. There are two major errors in swing-plane alignment. One error is the ____ swing, and the other is the ____ swing.

a. pumphandle, stretched
b. inward, outward
c. bumpout, wraparound
d. power, finesse

____ 16. In the delivery, your takeaway is moving your ____ from supporting the ____ in the ____ to a position out from the body, slightly down and toward the ____ .

a. bowling hand, ball, follow-through, front
b. balance hand, ball, pushaway, back
c. bowling hand, ball, slide, back
d. balance hand, sliding foot, slide, front

____ 17. If you do not keep your shoulders stable during your swing, your ideal swing plane will probably deviate, causing a bumpout swing, a wraparound swing, or a combination of both, called a ____ swing.

a. wrapout
b. bumparound
c. chicken wing
d. looped

____ 18. The lower your ball is placed into the swing, the ____ your backswing and the ____ your total swing time. The higher your ball is placed into the swing, the ____ your backswing and the ____ your total swing time.

a. higher, shorter, lower, longer
b. lower, longer, higher, shorter
c. lower, shorter, lower, shorter
d. lower, shorter, higher, longer

____ 19. The pendulum swing and the takeaway should begin on count

a. "AND" after "four."

b. "one."

c. "two."

d. "three."

____ 20. In executing the pushaway, ____ is as important as feel to ensure accuracy in placing the ball in line with the target.

a. a deep breath

b. the cadence

c. speed

d. visual feedback

____ 21. In the coordinated pushaway, pendulum swing, and takeaway movement, the back is ____ , the direction of the pushaway is ____ the shoulders and ____ the approach, and the takeaway is timed with the ____ .

a. upright, parallel with, vertical to, first step

b. upright, perpendicular to, horizontal with, first step

c. upright, perpendicular to, parallel with, ball

d. stooped, parallel with, parallel with, forward swing

____ 22. Proper timing of the pushaway with the swingside foot in the first step is necessary to create a

a. free pendulum swing.

b. rounded pushaway.

c. straight, upright posture.

d. sufficient amount of swing tension.

____ 23. When a bowler becomes excited, or "hyped," the most common reaction is for the pace of the ____ to increase. This condition, difficult for a bowler to sense, is called ____ ; it is characterized by the ball's being ____ with respect to the footwork, and it causes additional problems later in the delivery.

a. footwork, late feet, early

b. armswing, fast arm, late

c. pushaway, fast push, late

d. footwork, fast feet, late

____ 24. In coordinating the pushaway with the swingside foot it is important to

a. walk in a 'toe-heel" manner.

b. extend the elbows when the swingside heel touches down.

c. lock the knees before beginning movement.

d. extend the elbows when the balance-heel touches down.

____ 25. A(n) ____ pushaway can result in a hop between the second and third steps (in the four-step delivery), causing your ball to arrive at the foul line before your sliding foot, as well as a loss of lift with your fingers at the release.

a. properly timed

b. late

c. early

d. coordinated

____ 26. Proper footwork does not allow for a premature bend of your knees. In order to execute the footwork properly, you should

a. never bend your knees.

b. bend your knees during your second step.

c. bend your knees on the count of "two."

d. bend your knees after the count of "three."

____ 27. In executing a proper pushaway, begin a crisp push and a slow first step on the "AND"

a. after "one."

b. after "two."

c. before "four."

d. after "four."

____ 28. The most apparent effect of late pushaway (and resulting late ball) is a ____ forward swing and a ____ of your ball at the release.

a. hurried, smoothing

b. slow, pulling

c. hurried, pulling

d. smooth, sliding

____ 29. Proper footwork includes walking

a. with one foot directly in front of the other.

b. with one foot slightly crossing in front of the other.

c. with the feet approximately 3 inches apart.

d. with the feet approximately 1 inch apart.

____ 30. A well-executed finish allows more efficient projection of your ball onto the lane with more power because you use

a. the larger muscles of your arm and shoulder to apply lift.

b. the larger muscles of your back and legs to apply lift.

c. your head to control the movement of your propelling foot.

d. the forearm and thumb muscles to apply lift.

____ 31. For stability in the finish, your feet must be ____ , your shoulders and hips ____ your swing, and your back ____ as you are releasing your ball.

a. together, perpendicular to, upright

b. apart, perpendicular to, leaning forward

c. together, parallel with, upright

d. apart, perpendicular to, upright

____ 32. The most apparent effect of early pushaway (and resulting early ball) is a ____ of the ball at the top of your backswing and a ____ of your ball at the release.

a. floating, smoothing

b. slowness, pulling

c. floating, dumping

d. smooth, sliding

____ 33. Your body orientation at recovery (after the slide) may be compared to either a skier landing after a distance jump or of a fencer during a lunge. This posture is termed "sitting tall," and is characterized by no more than ____ degrees of forward lean of the upper body.

a. 20

b. 30

c. 45

d. 60

____ 34. *Ball dynamics* refers to the collective ____ and ____ motions of a bowling ball as it proceeds down the lane toward the pins. The way a ball visibly acts on the lane is termed a ____ .

a. touchdown, tracking, full-roller

b. skidding, rolling, ball reaction

c. skidding, rolling, track

d. to, fro, track

____ 35. When would a straight ball be preferable to a hook ball?

a. when lane conditions are difficult

b. on the first ball of every frame

c. when you want the steepest angle into the pocket

d. when you are an advanced bowler

____ 36. Why may a bowler have difficulty maintaining traction with the swingside foot during the finish?

a. the sole of the sliding shoe is made of rubber

b. the heel of either shoe is made of rubber

c. the sole of the swingside shoe is made of leather

d. the sole of the sliding shoe is made of leather

____ 37. Why is a hook ball the best strike ball?

a. It has a steeper angle of attack to the pocket.

b. It has less spin than a straight ball.

c. It is easier to roll than a straight ball.

d. It is more sensitive to variations in the lane condition.

____ 38. A targeting system helps you maintain superior execution from shot to shot because it

a. eliminates the need for aiming at a place on the lane.

b. preserves the parallel relationship between the approach and target lines.

c. allows you to look right at the pins as you release the ball.

d. preserves the perpendicular relationship between the approach and target lines.

____ 39. You should use the hook ball for ____ whenever possible and the straight ball for ____ . However, either could be used for strikes and spares on a ____ lane.

a. strikes, spares, poorly maintained

b. spares, strikes, well-maintained

c. strikes, spares, uniform-friction

d. spares, strikes, uniform-friction

____ 40. If your ball veers off to one side when you attempt to roll a straight ball, you may assume that

a. your fingers are not being held at 12 o'clock.
b. you muscled the ball.
c. lane conditions are spotty.
d. your fingers are being held at 12 o'clock.

____ 41. Left-handed bowlers count boards from ____ to ____ ; right-handed bowlers count from ____ to ____ .

a. inside, outside, inside, outside
b. outside, inside, outside, inside
c. right, left, left, right
d. right, left, right, left

____ 42. The term "having the fingers in the shot" refers to the feel of

a. the fingers in the fingerholes during the setup.
b. the fingers squeezing the grip during the swing.
c. the fingers lifting, or projecting, the ball onto the lane.
d. the fingers feeling pain after bowling for several hours.

____ 43. Strikes are obtained by directing accurate, well-executed ____ toward intelligently selected ____ on the lane.

a. shots, pins
b. gazes, pins
c. deliveries, pins
d. shots, targets

____ 44. The distance in boards between your sliding foot and the point of contact of your ball at or near the foul line can also be considered the horizontal distance between your body's center of gravity and the center of your ball. This space is also called the

a. placement distance.
b. placement deflection.
c. pocket distance.
d. pocket deflection.

____ 45. In evaluating a target line, if you are *not* executing properly, you should

a. make target line adjustments on every ball until you are striking.
b. make target line adjustments 1 board at a time.
c. not make any target line adjustments, even if you are correctly executing.
d. not make any target line adjustments until you have corrected your execution.

____ 46. If your ball hits the desired target point but misses the strike pocket to the outside, you should

a. move your setup location to the inside, 2 boards at a time.
b. move your setup location to the outside, 2 boards at a time.
c. not move your setup location.
d. move your setup location closer to the foul line.

____ 47. The ideal board number of the strike pocket is

a. 17 for a right-hander and 24 for a left-hander.

b. irrelevant because many different impact points result in strikes.

c. variable, depending on the amount of dressing used on the lane.

d. 17.

____ 48. The foul line is ____ feet from the headpin, and the arrows are approximately ____ feet from the foul line. Therefore, the arrows are approximately ____ feet from the headpin.

a. 6; 30, 30

b. 60, 15, 45

c. 50, 20, 30

d. 50, 15, 35

____ 49. You must always try to walk parallel with your target line,

a. unless you are attempting a spare.

b. even if that target line requires you to walk at an angle to the foul line.

c. unless you find that you are walking away from the pocket.

d. unless you are trying to pick up a corner pin.

____ 50. Spare targeting is identical with strike targeting, except that the ____ changes with each spare leave.

a. visual target

b. pin impact point

c. touchdown point

d. target point

____ 51. In moving the setup location on the approach or the visual target on the lane, a "change" means the number of boards different from your strike target line positions. A +8 move of your feet in your setup location means that you would move your feet 8 boards ____ your ____ channel than the strike setup location. A −5 move means that you would move 5 boards ____ the ____ channel than your strike setup location.

a. farther from, balance-side, closer to, balance-side

b. farther from, swingside, farther from, swingside

c. farther from, swingside, closer to, swingside

d. closer to, swingside, farther from, swingside

____ 52. What are the most important things you should consider when selecting your bowling ball (house ball)?

a. fingerhole size, span, and ball weight

b. fingerhole size, ball weight, and the angles of the fingerholes and thumbholes

c. thumbhole size, span, and ball weight

d. thumbhole size, ball weight, and the angles of the fingerholes and thumbholes

_____ 53. In the first frame, you get 8 pins on your first ball, then convert your spare. In the second frame, you get a channel ball on your first ball and 7 pins on your second ball. What is your score in the first frame?

a. 8
b. 10
c. 15
d. 17

_____ 54. Which pin is commonly called the kingpin?

a. 1 pin
b. 3 pin
c. 5 pin
d. 7 pin

NAME	1	2	3	4	5	6	7	8	9	10
Kim	6 2	7 /	X	9 –	8 /	7 /	X	X	X	9 / 8

_____ 55. What is the correct score for this game?

a. 190
b. 161
c. 95
d. 182

_____ 56. Bowler A's average is 150. Bowler B's average is 130. Using the percentage difference method with 80%, what handicap is given?

a. bowler A gets 104 pins
b. bowler B gets 120 pins
c. bowler A gets 16 pins
d. bowler B gets 16 pins

_____ 57. Which is the most effective type of alignment for getting strikes and spares?

a. pin bowling
b. spot bowling
c. target line bowing
d. line bowling

_____ 58. How are lane boards numbered?

a. from right to left
b. from left to right
c. from outside to inside
d. from inside to outside

_____ 59. What is meant by an 8-to-10 target line?

a. You release your ball on board 8 aiming for a target point on board 10.
b. You release your ball on board 10 aiming for a target point on board 8.
c. You aim for a target point on board 8 and hit the pins at board 10.
d. You release your ball on board 8 and hit the pins at board 10.

____ 60. What is the proper impact point for a strike?

a. Board 17 for a right-handed bowler.
b. Board 25 for a left-handed bowler.
c. Board 17 for all bowlers.
d. Board 25 for all bowlers.

____ 61. Which principle best describes spare targeting?

a. If your spare leave is to the outside, move your setup location to the inside.
b. If your spare leave is to the inside, move your setup location to the inside.
c. No matter where your spare leave is, never move your setup location.
d. Move your setup location only for 7- and 10-pin leaves.

____ 62. If you leave the 2, 4, and 5 pins, which pin(s) should be your primary impact pin(s)?

a. all 3 pins
b. the 2 pin
c. the 4 pin
d. the 5 pin

____ 63. If you leave the 6 and 10 pins, which pin(s) should be your primary impact pin(s)?

a. 6 pin
b. 10 pin
c. both pins
d. 3 pin

____ 64. If you leave the 1, 3, 6, and 10 pins, which pin(s) should be your primary impact pin(s)?

a. 6 pin
b. 3 pin
c. 1-2 pins
d. 1-3 pins

____ 65. If you leave the 5 and 10 pins, which pin(s) should be your translated primary impact pin(s)?

a. 5 pin
b. 10 pin
c. 2 pin
d. 3 pin

____ 66. If your ball begins to miss the pocket, even though you are consistently hitting your successful target line, then the first element you should analyze is your ____ .

a. visual target
b. execution
c. target line
d. target point

____ 67. Which statement best describes the relationship between the length of your bowling arm and the speed of your footwork?

a. The shorter the arm, the faster the footwork must be.

b. The longer the arm, the faster the footwork must be.

c. The speed of the footwork depends upon leg length, not arm length.

d. There is no relationship between arm length and speed of footwork.

____ 68. Which statement best describes how fast you should roll a hook ball?

a. Always try to roll your hook ball slower than your straight ball.

b. Always try to roll your hook ball faster than your straight ball.

c. Always try to roll your hook ball the same speed as your straight ball.

d. Because your straight ball spins less, it will always be faster than your hook ball no matter what you do.

____ 69. Goals should be challenging but realistic; they should be ____ goals rather than ____ goals. Some ____ -range goals should be used as mirrors of progress in the attainment of ____ -range goals. Furthermore, goals should be stated specifically, positively, and in the ____ voice.

a. performance, outcome, short, long, passive

b. outcome, performance, short, long, active

c. performance, outcome, short, long, active

d. outcome, performance, long, short, passive

____ 70. Two synonyms for mental practice are

a. mental discipline and solo mental.

b. mental imagery and mental rehearsal.

c. buddy system and solo mental.

d. mental system and reciprocal.

____ 71. Which statement about practice is most correct?

a. Mental practice has very little effect on bowling performance.

b. Mental practice improves skill more than physical practice does.

c. Physical practice works only for beginners.

d. A combination of mental and physical practice leads to optimal performance.

____ 72. Why is the buddy-system of practice useful?

a. It is less boring than solo practice.

b. The bowler can compare the feel of the shot with the observer's verbal feedback.

c. It's more like league bowling than solo practice is.

d. The bowler can associate observer feedback with a third bowler's performance.

____ 73. Mental practice involves creating a perfect-performance experience in your "mind's eye." The technique allows you to

a. sit in a quiet room and read about bowling.

b. review your delivery without actually bowling.

c. give up physical practice but still improve.

d. improve your physiological balance and tone.

____ 74. During mental practice, it is important to
- a. exclude all senses normally associated with a real setting.
- b. picture both errors and correct performance.
- c. make your image as vivid as possible with regard to the senses.
- d. picture only errors.

____ 75. An example of a beneficial short-term goal is
- a. root for the opposing team.
- b. become league champions.
- c. improve your average 10 pins in a year's time.
- d. make the best and most consistent shots possible.

____ 76. If you get a strike on the first ball in the 10th frame, what happens?
- a. You are finished with the game.
- b. You get to roll 2 more balls.
- c. You get to bowl 2 more frames.
- d. You get to add 20 pins to your score.

____ 77. What is the proper term for a ball that veers from the bowler's inside to the outside?
- a. hook
- b. curve
- c. slider
- d. backup

____ 78. If your foot slides across the foul line as you deliver your first ball, what happens?
- a. You receive 0 pins on your first ball and automatically lose your second ball.
- b. You receive 0 pins on your first ball, reset the pins, and bowl your second ball at a full rack.
- c. You receive 0 pins on your first ball and throw your second ball at the remaining pins.
- d. You receive the number of pins you knock down, but you lose your second ball.

____ 79. ____ Doubles is competition in which one partner bowls the spare leaves of the other. ____ Doubles requires that a partner wait until his or her partner bowls the first ball of their frame in order to see whether a higher pin count can be obtained.
- a. MacLachlan, Hungarian
- b. Nassau, Skins
- c. Scotch, Best Ball
- d. Best Ball, Scotch

____ 80. For which of the following spare conversions would a left-handed bowler *not* roll a strike ball?
- a. 2-5
- b. 1-2-4-7
- c. 5-8
- d. 3-5

WRITTEN EXAMINATION ANSWERS

1. a
2. d
3. b
4. d
5. d
6. a
7. c
8. a
9. d
10. a
11. b
12. d
13. b
14. d
15. c
16. b
17. d
18. d
19. b
20. d
21. c
22. a
23. d
24. b
25. c
26. d
27. d
28. c
29. c
30. b
31. d
32. c
33. a
34. b
35. a
36. c
37. a
38. b
39. a
40. a
41. b
42. c
43. d
44. a
45. d
46. b
47. d
48. b
49. b
50. b
51. c
52. c
53. b
54. c
55. a
56. d
57. c
58. c
59. a
60. c
61. a
62. b
63. a
64. d
65. c
66. b
67. a
68. c
69. c
70. b
71. d
72. b
73. b
74. c
75. d
76. b
77. d
78. b
79. c
80. d

Completed Gameline for Question 55

NAME	1	2	3	4	5	6	7	8	9	10
Kim	6 2 8	7 / 28	X 47	9 – 56	8 / 73	7 / 93	X 123	X 152	X 172	9 / 8 190

Appendices

Appendix A
How to Use the Knowledge Structure Overview

A knowledge structure is an instructional tool; by completing one, you make a very personal statement about your knowledge of a subject and how that knowledge guides your decisions in teaching and coaching. The knowledge structure for bowling outlined here has been designed for a teaching environment, with teaching progressions that emphasize technique and performance objectives in realistic settings. In a coaching environment, you would need to emphasize more physiological and conditioning factors with training progressions.

The Knowledge Structure of Bowling shows the first page, or an *overview* of a completed knowledge structure. The knowledge structure is divided into broad categories of information that are used for all of the participant and instructor guides in the Steps to Success Activity Series. Those categories are

- physiological training and conditioning,
- background knowledge,
- psychomotor skills and tactics, and
- psycho-social concepts.

Physiological training and conditioning has several subcategories, including warm-up and cool-down. Research in exercise physiology and the medical sciences has demonstrated the importance of warming-up before and cooling-down after physical activity. The participant and instructor guides present principles and exercises for effective warm-up and cool-down, which, because of time restrictions, are usually the only training activities done in the teaching environment. In a more intense coaching environment, additional categories should be added—training principles, injury prevention, training progressions, and nutrition principles.

The background-knowledge category presents subcategories of information that represent essential background knowledge that all instructors should command when meeting their classes. Bowling background knowledge includes the sport of bowling, safety, basic rules and scoring, and selecting your equipment.

Under psychomotor skills and tactics, all the individual skills in an activity are named. For bowling, these are shown as the setup, pendulum swing, footwork, utility delivery, ball dynamics, strike targeting, refinement, and spare targeting. These skills are presented in a recommended order of presentation. In a complete knowledge structure, each skill is broken down into subskills delineating selected technical, biomechanical, motor learning, and other teaching and coaching points that describe mature performance. These points can be found in the Student Keys to Success or in the Keys to Success Checklists within the participant's book.

Once individual skills are identified and analyzed, then selected strategies (decision-making situations) of the activity are also identified and analyzed. For bowling, the tactics include goal setting and practicing for success. Notice that they are arranged to reflect the decision-making strategies and capabilities of learners as they become more proficient.

The psycho-social category identifies selected concepts from the sport psychology and sociology literature that have been shown to contribute to the learners' understanding of and success in the activity. These concepts are built into the key concepts and activities for teaching. For bowling, the concept identified is mental discipline.

In order to be a successful teacher or coach, you must convert what you have learned as a student or done as a player or performer to a form of knowing that is both conscious and appropriate for presentation to others. A knowledge structure helps you with this transition and speeds your *steps to success.* You should view a knowledge structure as the most basic level of teaching knowledge you possess for a sport or an activity. For more information on how to develop your own knowledge structure, see the textbook that accompanies this series, *Instructional Design for Teaching Physical Activities.*

Knowledge Structure of Bowling (Overview)

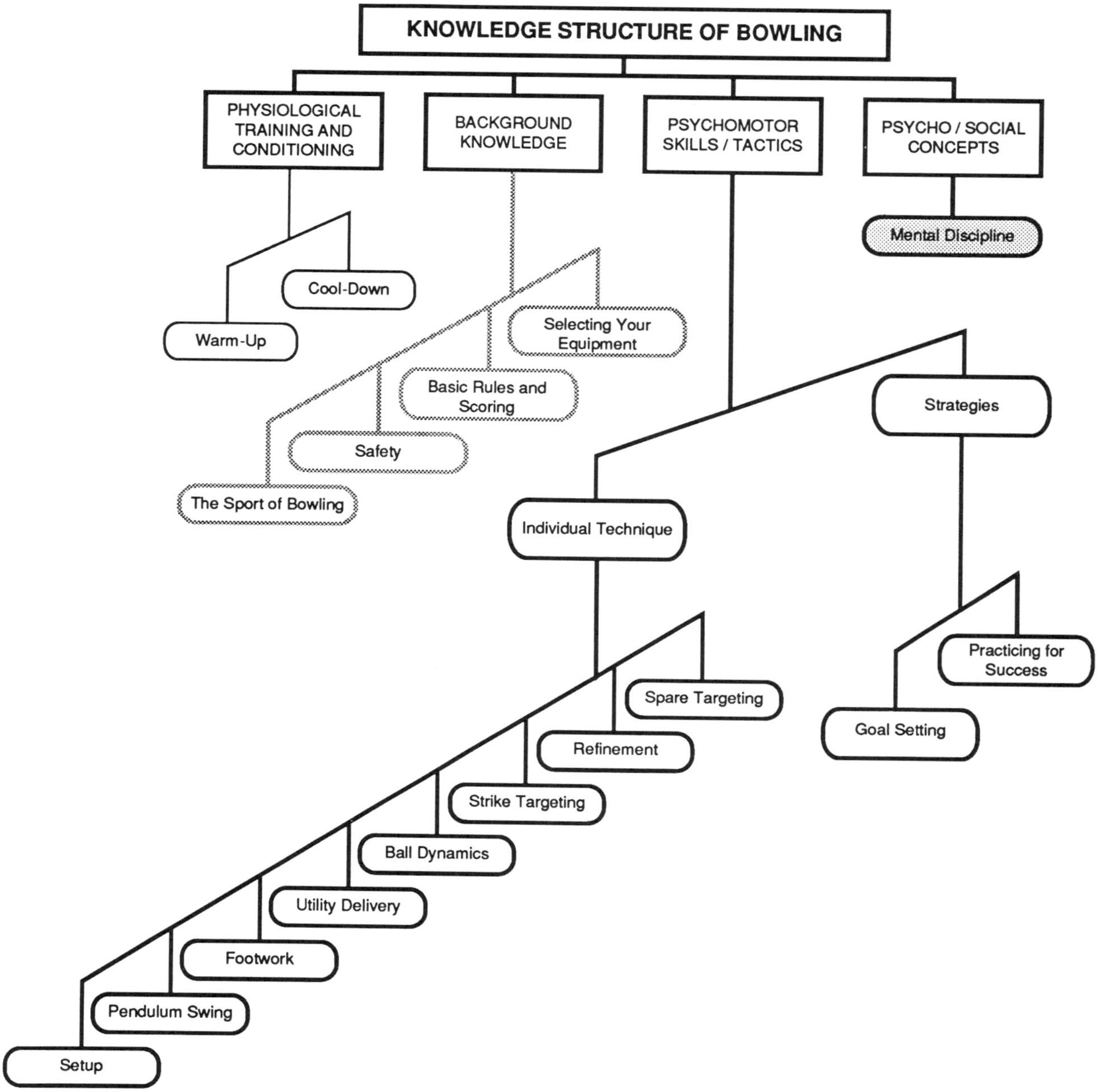

Note. From "The Role of Expert Knowledge Structures in an Instructional Design Model for Physical Education" by J.N. Vickers, 1983, *Journal of Teaching in Physical Education*, **2**(3), pp. 25, 27. Copyright 1983 by Joan N. Vickers. Adapted by permission. This Knowledge Structure of Bowling was designed specifically for the Steps to Success Activity Series by Joan N. Vickers, Judy P. Wright, and Robert H. Strickland.

Appendix B.1

Sample Scope and Teaching Sequence

N New **R** Review **C** Continue **P** Student Directed Practice

NAME OF ACTIVITY Bowling

LEVEL OF LEARNER Beginning–Intermediate

Steps	Session Number	1	2	3	4	5	6	7	8	9	10	11	12	13	14	15	16	17	18	19	20	21	22	23	24	25	26	27	28	29	30
1	Setup	N	R	C	P	P	P	P	P	P	P	P	P	P	P	P	P	P	P	P	P	P	P	P	P	P	P	P	P	P	P
2	Pendulum Swing		N	R	C	P	P	P	P	P	P	P	P	P	P	P	P	P	P	P	P	P	P	P	P	P	P	P	P	P	P
3	Footwork			N	R	C	P	P	P	P	P	P	P	P	P	P	P	P	P	P	P	P	P	P	P	P	P	P	P	P	P
4	Utility Delivery			N	R	C	P	P	P	P	P	P	P	P	P	P	P	P	P	P	P	P	P	P	P	P	P	P	P	P	P
5	Ball Dynamics				N	R	C	P	P	P	P	P	P	P	P	P	P	P	P	P	P	P	P	P	P	P	P	P	P	P	P
6	Strike Targeting						N	R	C	C	C	P	P	P	P	P	P	P	P	P	P	P	P	P	P	P	P	P	P	P	P
7	Refine Swing and Takeaway											N	R	C	P	P	P	P	P	P	P	P	P	P	P	P	P	P	P	P	P
8	Refine Your Pushaway												N	R	C	P	P	P	P	P	P	P	P	P	P	P	P	P	P	P	P
9	Refine Three Skills													N	R	C	P	P	P	P	P	P	P	P	P	P	P	P	P	P	P
10	Refine First Step and Pushaway														N	R	C	P	P	P	P	P	P	P	P	P	P	P	P	P	P
11	Refine Four Skills															N	R	C	P	P	P	P	P	P	P	P	P	P	P	P	P
12	Finish																N	R	C	P	P	P	P	P	P	P	P	P	P	P	P
13	Refine Five Skills																	N	R	C	P	P	P	P	P	P	P	P	P	P	P
14	Spare Targeting																		N	R	C	C	C	C	C	C	C	C	C	C	C
15	Goal Setting																								N	R	P	P	P	P	P
16	Practicing for Success																											N	P	P	P
17																															
18																															
19																															
20																															
21																															
22																															
23																															
24																															
25																															

Notes:

Appendix B.2
How to Use the Scope and Teaching Sequence Form

A completed Scope and Teaching Sequence is, in effect, a master lesson plan. It lists all the individual skills to be included in your course, recorded (vertically) in the progressive sequence in which you have decided to present them and showing (horizontally) the manner and the sessions in which you teach them.

The Sample Scope and Teaching Sequence illustrates how the chart is to be used. This chart indicates that in session 4, the class will practice the setup (Step 1), continue learning the pendulum swing (Step 2), review footwork (Step 3) and the utility delivery (Step 4), and be introduced to ball dynamics (Step 5). It also indicates that the skills in Step 4 (Utility Delivery), for example, are new during session 3, reviewed in session 4, continued in session 5, and practiced further during the remaining sessions available.

A course Scope and Teaching Sequence chart (use the blank form in Appendix B.2) will help you to better plan your daily teaching strategies (see Appendix D.1). It will take some experience to accurately predict how much material you can cover in each session, but by completing a plan like this, you can compare your progress to your plan and revise the plan to better fit the next class.

The chart will also help you tailor the amount of material to the length of time you have to teach it. Be sure that your course's Scope and Teaching Sequence allots ample time for review and practice of each area. Notice that the materials covered in Steps 15 and 16 may be used as supplemental assignments at any time throughout the course, or they may be reserved for intermediate-level students. In addition, some of the later activities may be used for variety once you have taught strike-targeting techniques; for example, the drill, Bowling Bingo (Step 14, Drill 12), is a fun game that uses only first ball attempts.

Remember that the Scope and Teaching Sequence can be affected by the number of students in a class, the abilities of the students, and the number of lanes and bowling balls available. Whether you use the sample presented here or one you complete for yourself, as a guideline, it will be very difficult to follow either of them exactly. Be ready to make adjustments according to the variables mentioned.

Appendix B.2

Scope and Teaching Sequence

NAME OF ACTIVITY ____________

LEVEL OF LEARNER ____________

New [N] Review [R] Continue [C] Student Directed Practice [P]

Steps	Session Number	1	2	3	4	5	6	7	8	9	10	11	12	13	14	15	16	17	18	19	20	21	22	23	24	25	26	27	28	29	30
1																															
2																															
3																															
4																															
5																															
6																															
7																															
8																															
9																															
10																															
11																															
12																															
13																															
14																															
15																															
16																															
17																															
18																															
19																															
20																															
21																															
22																															
23																															
24																															
25																															

Note. From *Badminton: A Structures of Knowledge Approach* (pp. 60-61) by J.N. Vickers and D. Brecht, 1987, Calgary, AB: University Printing Services. Copyright 1987 by Joan N. Vickers. Adapted by permission.

Appendix C.1

Sample Individual Program

INDIVIDUAL COURSE IN Bowling GRADE/COURSE SECTION Beginning

STUDENT'S NAME ____________ STUDENT ID # ____________

	SKILLS/CONCEPTS	TECHNIQUE AND PERFORMANCE OBJECTIVES	WT* × %	POINT PROGRESS** = 1	2	3	4	FINAL SCORE***
	Finished Delivery	*Technique*: Correct setup, pendulum swing, pushaway, takeaway, footwork, and finish.	3.0					
		Performance 1: Average score for 20 games bowled.	1.0	90–99	100–109	110–119	120+	
		Performance 2: Number of times hit strike target.	1.0	12/20	14/20	16/20	18/20	
		Performance 3: Percentage of spare conversions out of possible attempts.	1.0	60	70	80	90	
	Lane Etiquette	*Performance*: Checks for clearance, yeilds right of way, does not distract other bowlers, uses only purposeful movements on approach.	1.0	12/20	14/20	16/20	18/20	
	Written Exam	*Performance*: Percentage scored out of possible points.	3.0	60	70	80	90	

*WT = Weighting of an objective's degree of difficulty.

**PROGRESS = Ongoing success, which may be expressed in terms of (a) accumulated points (1, 2, 3, 4); (b) grades (D, C, B, A); (c) symbols (merit, bronze, silver, gold); (d) unsatisfactory/satisfactory; percentages; and others as desired.

***FINAL SCORE equals WT times PROGRESS.

Appendix C.2

Individual Program

INDIVIDUAL COURSE IN ______________________ GRADE/COURSE SECTION ______________

STUDENT'S NAME ______________________ STUDENT ID # ______________

SKILLS/CONCEPTS		TECHNIQUE AND PERFORMANCE OBJECTIVES	WT* ×	POINT PROGRESS**			=	FINAL SCORE***
			%	1	2	3	4	

Note. From "The Role of Expert Knowledge Structures in an Instructional Design Model for Physical Education" by J.N. Vickers, 1983, *Journal of Teaching in Physical Education*, **2**(3), p. 17. Copyright 1983 by Joan N. Vickers. Adapted by permission.

*WT = Weighting of an objective's degree of difficulty.

**PROGRESS = Ongoing success, which may be expressed in terms of (a) accumulated points (1, 2, 3, 4); (b) grades (D, C, B, A); (c) symbols (merit, bronze, silver, gold); (d) unsatisfactory/satisfactory; and others as desired.

***FINAL SCORE equals WT times PROGRESS.

Appendix C.2
How to Use the Individual Program Form

To complete an individual program for each student, you must first make five decisions about evaluation:

1. How many skills or concepts can you or should you evaluate, considering the number of students and the time available? The larger your classes and the shorter your class length, the fewer objectives you will be able to use.
2. What specific quantitative or qualitative criteria will you use to evaluate specific skills? See the Sample Individual Program (Appendix C.1) for ideas.
3. What relative weight is to be assigned to each specific skill, considering its importance in the course and the amount of practice time available?
4. What type of grading system do you wish to use? Will you use letters, (A, B, C, D), satisfactory/unsatisfactory, a number or point system (1, 2, 3, etc.), or percentages? Or, do you prefer a system of achievement levels such as colors (red, white, blue), or medallions (bronze, silver, gold)?
5. Who will do the evaluating? You may want to delegate certain quantitative evaluations to be made by the students' peers up to a predetermined skill level (e.g., a ''B'' grade), with all qualitative evaluations and all top-grade determinations being made by you.

Once you have made these decisions, draw up an evaluation sheet (using Appendix C.2) that will fit the majority of your class members. Then decide whether you will establish a minimum passing score. Calculate this score and the maximum attainable score, and divide the difference into as many grade categories as you wish. If you use an achievement-level system, assign a numerical value to each level for your calculations.

The blank Individual Program form, as shown in Appendix C.2, is not intended to be used verbatim (although you may do so if you wish), but rather to suggest ideas that you can use, adapt, and integrate with your own ideas to tailor your program to you and your students.

Make copies of your program evaluation system to hand out to each student at your first class meeting, and be prepared to make modifications for those who need special consideration. Such modifications could include changing the weight assigned to particular skills for certain students, or substituting some skills for others, or varying the criteria used for evaluating selected students. Thus, individual differences can be recognized within your class.

You, the instructor, have the freedom to make the decisions about evaluating your students. Be creative. The best teachers always are.

Appendix D.1
Sample Lesson Plan

Lesson plan 3 of 30 Activity: Beginning Bowling

Class 10:00 - 11:20 TT

Objectives:

1. Continue proper setup.
2. Review pendulum swing.
3. Teach footwork and utility delivery.

Skill or concept	Learning activity	Teaching points
1. Distribute equipment	• Get shoes and ball	• Get your equipment as soon as you get to class
2. Warm-up	• See ''Preparing Your Body for Success''	• Warm-up on your own as soon as you get your equipment
3. Review pendulum swing	• Mimic pendulum swing without ball • Cue 10 repetitions	Review major cues: • Body squared and stable • Ball falls into swing • Body stable as ball swings and stops
4. Teach footwork without delivery	• Coordinate footwork and cadence (Step 3, Drill 2)	Identify major cues: • Upright and squared body before movement • Proper setup position • Heel-to-toe steps in cadence • Slide to sitting-tall finish
5. Teach utility delivery	• Mimic without a ball • Delivery with a ball (Step 4 Drill)	Identify major cues: • Normal setup • Count cadence • Push ball before ''one'' • Step forward before ''one'' • Elbows straight and swingside heel down on ''one'' • Let ball fall • Ball low on ''two'' • Ball high on ''three'' • Sliding sole down on ''four'' • Back upright • Release ball • Follow through
6. Closure and bridge to next class	• Ask class review questions • Relate activities of this class to next	
7. Cool down	• See ''Preparing Your Body for Success''	• Cool down on your own
8. Return equipment		• Return equipment on your own

Appendix D.2
How to Use the Lesson Plan Form

All teachers have learned in their training that lesson plans are vital to good teaching. This is a commonly accepted axiom, but there are many variations in the form that lesson plans can take. An effective lesson plan sets forth the objectives to be attained or attempted during the session. If there is no objective, there is no reason for teaching, and no basis for judging whether the teaching is effective.

Once you have named your objectives, list specific activities that will lead to attaining each. Every activity must be described in detail—what will take place and in what order, and how the class will be organized for the optimum learning situation. Record key words or phrases as focal points, as well as brief reminders of the applicable safety precautions.

Once you know your class size, number of lanes available, and student skill levels, set a time schedule that allocates a segment of the lesson for each activity to guide you in keeping to your plan. It is wise to also include in your lesson plan a list of all the equipment you will need, as well as a reminder to check for availability and location of the equipment before class.

An organized, professional approach to teaching requires preparing daily lesson plans. Each lesson plan provides you with an effective overview of your intended instruction and a means to evaluate it when class is over. Having lesson plans on file allows someone else to teach in your absence. You may modify the blank Lesson Plan form shown in Appendix D.2 to fit your own needs.

Lesson Plan

LESSON PLAN ________ OF ________

ACTIVITY ____________________

CLASS ____________________

OBJECTIVES:

SKILL OR CONCEPT	LEARNING ACTIVITIES	TEACHING POINTS	TIME

Note. From *Badminton: A Structures of Knowledge Approach* (p. 95) by J.N. Vickers and D. Brecht, 1987, Calgary, AB: University Printing Services.

References

Goc-Karp, G. , & Zakrajsek, D.B. (1987). Planning for learning: Theory into practice. *Journal of Teaching in Physical Education*, **6**(4), 377-392.

Housner, L.D., & Griffey, D.C. (1985). Teacher cognition: Differences in planning and interactive decision making between experienced and inexperienced teachers. *Research Quarterly for Exercise and Sport*, **56**(1), 45-53.

Imwold, C.H., & Hoffman, S.J. (1983). Visual recognition of a gymnastic skill by experienced and inexperienced instructors. *Research Quarterly for Exercise and Sport*, **54**(2), 149-155.

Powers, W. (1986). *The competitive edge*. Denton: Texas Training and Development Systems.

Suggested Readings

Allen, G., & Ritger, D. (1981). *The complete guide to bowling strikes*. Tempe, AZ: Tempe.

Boucher, S.H., & Rotella, R.J. (1987). A psychological skills educational program for closed-skill performance enhancement. *The Sport Psychologist*, **1**, 127-137.

Picchietti, R. (1981). *Lane conditions for bowlers*. Deerfield, IL: Tech-Ed.

Ritger, D., & Allen, G. (1978). *The complete guide to bowling spares*. Tempe, AZ: Ritger Sports.

Strickland, R. (1980). *Perceptive bowling*. Duncanville, TX: Professional Sports Services.

Taylor, B. (1956). *Target lines*. San Gabriel, CA: BT Bowling Products.

Taylor, B. (1970). *Fitting and drilling a bowling ball*. San Gabriel, CA: BT Bowling Products.

Taylor, B. (1973). *What really happened to Don Carter?* San Gabriel, CA: BT Bowling Products.

Taylor, B. (1974). *Balance*. San Gabriel, CA: BT Bowling Products.

Weber, D., & Alexander, R. (1981). *Weber on bowling*. Englewood Cliffs, NJ: Prentice-Hall.

Weiskopf, H. (1978). *The perfect game*. Englewood Cliffs, NJ: Prentice-Hall.

Welu, B., & Levine, J. (1972). *Add 30 pins to your bowling score*. New York: Crown.

Williams, J.W. (Ed.) (1986). *Applied sport psychology: Personal growth to peak performance*. Palo Alto, CA: Mayfield.